TEACHING LITERATURE IN MIDDLE SCHOOL: FICTION

Standards Consensus Series

National Council of Teachers of English
1111 W. Kenyon Road, Urbana, Illinois 61801-1096

Production Editor: Jamie Hutchinson

Series Cover Design and Interior Design: Joellen Bryant

NCTE Stock Number 52856-3050

It is the policy of NCTE in its journals and other publications to provide
a forum for the open discussion of ideas concerning the content and the
teaching of English and the language arts. Publicity accorded to any
particular point of view does not imply endorsement by the Executive
Committee, the Board of Directors, or the membership at large, except
in announcements of policy, where such endorsement is clearly speci-
fied.

Library of Congress Cataloging-in-Publication Data

Teaching literature in middle school: fiction.
      p.   cm. — (Standards consensus series)
NCTE Stock Number 52856-3050.
Includes bibliographical references.
ISBN 0-8141-5285-6
  1. Literature—Study and teaching (Secondary) I. National
Council of Teachers of English. II. Series.
PN59. T43 1996
808.3'071'2—dc20   95-49420
                                              CIP

CONTENTS

INTRODUCTION

RATIONALE FOR THE STANDARDS CONSENSUS SERIES

Much attention is given to matters that divide the teaching profession. But when NCTE collected dozens of standards statements, curriculum frameworks, and other key state curriculum documents in order to prepare *State of the States: A Report on English Language Arts Content Standards in Each State,* considerable agreement was evident in many areas of English language arts instruction. Similar consensus has been demonstrated in the development of the NCTE/IRA *Standards for the English Language Arts,* the core document that outlines national standards in our discipline.

A heartening fact has emerged from the standards movement, as varied as that movement has been: We are after all a community of teachers who draw upon shared instructional traditions in literature, composition, language, and related areas. Furthermore, in recent years the insight and invention of teachers and teacher educators have built upon those traditions in fascinating ways. The result is a rich body of practice-oriented material that parallels the mounting consensus in the profession.

NCTE has developed the Standards Consensus Series, then, in recognition of the existence of core beliefs about English language arts as revealed in innumerable standards-related documents and classroom ideas generated by teachers. The assumption underlying the series—and illustrated in it—is that good teachers have long been carrying out English language arts programs and classroom activities that exemplify sound implementation of the commonly held standards. The contents of each volume in the Standards Consensus Series were selected mainly from a database of classroom-practice materials. The database materials had been selected by teachers from a larger body of writings previously published by NCTE, mainly in the popular *NOTES Plus* journal.

In this volume we have gathered exciting activities that draw students into the wider worlds created in literature. The high value that our profession places on such encounters is plain from the sampling of standards documents quoted below:

> *South Carolina*—Students become familiar with the rich cultural heritage of language through experiences with literature. By reading and personally responding to a variety of genres, the learner develops into a lifelong and selective reader who enjoys a wide variety of literature. (15–16)

Colorado—Students read and recognize literature as an expression of human experience. (4)

Michigan—Students will explore and respond meaningfully to classic and contemporary literature and other texts from many cultures that have been recognized for their quality and/or literary merit. (25)

Massachusetts—Students connect literature to personal experience and contemporary issues. (67)

Alabama—Students will demonstrate knowledge of the types, periods, and characteristics of literature from diverse cultures and places. (n.p.)

North Dakota—The students analyze the ways in which specific pieces of literature have been influenced by the culture and time period; understand that the reader interacts with the text; understand how genre characteristics affect a given text. (31)

Arkansas—[Students will] read excellent works and authors from various genres and cultures; analyze how the works of a given period reflect historical events; understand the relationship between contemporary writing and past literary traditions; develop criteria for judging the quality of literary works. (5)

New York—Students learn a wide variety of literary concepts commonly used in reporting on and discussing literature, including genre (poetry, novel, drama, biography, fable, myth, legend), plot, setting, character, point of view, theme, meter, rhyme scheme, tragedy, and comedy. (22)

Alaska—Students will use . . . literature of many types and cultures . . . to understand self and others. (n.p.)

These varied and powerful expressions of belief in the importance of literature point to the usefulness of this collection of materials on fiction as a key volume in the Standards Consensus Series. Of course, this is not to suggest that this book is of value only to those seeking to establish relationships between standards and instructional practice. Every middle school teacher of English language arts will find a wealth of lively, academically well-grounded ideas in this volume. Even if there had been no "standards movement" as such, these materials would nonetheless present a profile of exemplary practice worthy of emulation in improving students' performance in English language arts.

Materials on exemplary practice in the teaching of fiction are especially important at the middle school level. The various fiction genres can be particulary inviting and absorbing to middle school students. Fiction can afford enjoyment that will lead to lifelong reading habits. It deals with abiding themes and key issues that have been concerns of humanity through the ages. It can evoke crisp personal responses from students and generate thoughtful interaction in small-group and whole-class discussion. It can stimulate sustained analysis and critical and imaginative thinking. It is frequently a gateway to research—not only in the academic sense but in the broader sense of intensive inquiry into the forms of literature and life. For these reasons, the study of fiction was selected as the first literature-based volume for middle school in the Standards Consensus Series.

A few comments about the nature of the materials and their organization are in order. Consistent with NCTE position statements and with the texts of many standards documents, most of the classroom practices here do not isolate the teaching of literature as if it were unrelated to the entire range of English language arts skills and topics. The materials in the Standards Consensus Series demonstrate amply that good teachers often do everything at once—asking students to reflect upon and talk about literary experiences, encouraging them to make notes about their readings and discussions in preparation for writing, and finding other ways to weave the language arts together in an integral learning experience.

A North Carolina goals document makes this point especially well: "Communication is an interactive process that brings together the communicator(s), the activity or task, and the situation that surrounds them. It is a constructive, dynamic process, not an isolated event or an assembly of a set of sub-skills. . . . Though listed separately, the [North Carolina] goals are not to be perceived as linear or isolated entities. The goals are interrelated aspects of the dynamic process of communication" (46). While the focus of this volume is mainly on teaching fiction, then, the classroom experiences typically exemplify the dynamics of real teaching.

ORGANIZATION OF THIS BOOK

The materials in *Teaching Literature in Middle School: Fiction* are grouped in useful ways that will be described below. However, neither the arrangement of materials in this text nor the details of a particular classroom experience are intended to be prescriptive. The arrangement of the four sections is for convenience, not compartmentalization. There is no intention to isolate any particular aspect of the teaching of fiction from other aspects. Indeed, there is much fruitful overlapping of categories here; for example, "Engaging Students in Writing about Character" in Section 3 focuses on both response and character. The "Short Story Seminars" piece in the section on creating reading communities also deals with literary components.

As for the details of the classroom activities, teachers who use this book well will invariably translate the ideas in terms of their own experience. The day of know-all, tell-all books is past. Student populations differ; cookie-cutter activities simply don't work in every classroom environment. Most significant, teachers know their own students and they have sound intuitions about the kinds of ideas and materials that are and are not appropriate in their classrooms. From this solid collection of materials, teachers are invited to select, discard, amplify, adapt, and integrate ideas in light of the students they work with and know.

The first two sections of this volume focus largely on approaches to teaching fundamental components of fiction. **Section 1—Emphasis: Overview of Components, Exploring Character** begins with overviews of key literary components in fiction before moving on to articles that focus on a specific element—namely, character. Of course, middle school students are quite tuned into "sizing up" people, and the writers of the materials in this section provide ingenious ways of bringing their students to discussion and analysis of fictional characters. Among the highly motivational approaches are writing letters of recommendation for literary characters, composing dialogue, writing a character's "autobiography," and speculating about careers for characters.

Section 2—Emphasis: Theme provides help with a literary component that middle school students frequently grapple with in the study of fiction. The initial piece presents an unusual way of dealing with plot, but as Arlene Pullen points out in the next item, students who are asked, "But What Is the Story Really About?" will "invariably respond with plot summaries" rather than with exploration of a theme. Among the themes included in the chapter are problems faced by adolescents, such as family relations and the search for values, and social problems such as oppression of minorities and the uses of technology. And while Joan Kaywell reminds us that "we are English teachers, not guidance counselors," it remains true that literature-based discussion of the problems faced by adolescents can be uniquely rewarding and productive. Kaywell's article provides a thorough framework for such discussion in the middle school English class. The section ends with a unique prereading exercise aimed at making students' reading of a short story more interesting and perceptive.

More expansive and perhaps more challenging approaches make up the final two sections. **Section 3—Emphasis: From Response to Criticism** begins with an in-depth treatment of response-based instruction in Toni Cade Bambara's short story "Raymond's Run." This is followed by items that illustrate various ways in which middle school teachers can elicit insightful student response. The methods here go well beyond formulaic recitation and standard book reports, describing approaches such as literary dinner parties and the use of objects, colors, and music for articulation of student response. The last two items skillfully show how response-based teaching can be seamlessly joined with literary analysis and criticism, helping the student both to respond at a personal level and to decenter, moving toward literary critical perspectives.

The items in **Section 4—Emphasis: Creating Communities of Readers** deal with an important concern in middle school English language arts instruction—helping students to see themselves as readers and as participants in ongoing discussions about works they have read. The first entry is a teacher's reading inventory that takes a new tack, seeking to ensure that each student will enter the reading community with material tailored to his or her interests. This is followed by a bright array of items that promote various kinds of collaboration and community. Ideas are presented for helping students recommend books to each other; student self-selection followed by group study; using drama and role-playing to help break down barriers of prejudice; involvement of siblings and parents; student-initiated contact with authors and other adult role models; student seminars; and others. The section concludes with entries by Michael Kennedy and Linda Rief that involve sustained collaborative student effort, the first focused on adapting a novel into play form and the latter on integrating reading experiences with writing and music in the classroom.

The preparation of this volume revealed that many topics and concerns found in NCTE's previously published classroom practice materials on fiction closely parallel the foci of the state-level standards statements cited earlier in this introduction. In a time of considerable pessimism and discord in education, it is encouraging to find such grounds for consensus in the teaching of English and language arts. In the emerging state and national standards, we find *common goals* for the teaching of our discipline. In the reported practices of the English language arts teaching community, we find *a formidable body of ideas about how to achieve those goals.* The Standards Consensus Series is both a recognition of cohesiveness and a tool for growth in the profession.

Finally, some acknowledgments are in order. First, kudos to the teachers and teacher educators who contributed their thoughtful practices to this collection, mostly via past issues of NCTE's *NOTES Plus.* The texts from that periodical are virtually unchanged, and the institutional affiliations of the teachers reflect their teaching assignments at the time of original publication. A few entries in this volume are from non–middle school or non–junior high level (i.e., from high school teachers or teacher educators who work with middle school teachers), but all selections were judged to be appropriate for middle school use by the teachers who reviewed materials from the database.

Issues of *NOTES Plus* and other publications which were sources for this text have been regularly reviewed by chairs of the NCTE Secondary Section. These include the present chair, Joan Naomi Steiner, and former chairs Mildred Miller, Jackie Swensson, Faith Schullstrom, George B. Shea, Jr., Theodore Hipple, and Skip Nicholson. Staff coordinators and advisors for *NOTES Plus* have also been a key in this endeavor. The staff coordinator since 1985 has been Felice Kaufmann. The teachers who categorized the vast body of materials for inclusion in NCTE's general database of teaching practices are Carol Snyder and Jim Forman. This text was compiled by NCTE staff editor Jamie Hutchinson.

REFERENCES

Alabama Department of Education. n.d. *Learning Goals and Performance Objectives.*

Alaska Department of Education. 1994. *Alaska Student Performance Standards.*

Arkansas Department of Education. 1993. *Arkansas English Language Arts Curriculum Framework.*

[Colorado] Standards and Assessment Council. December 1994. *Model Content Standards for Reading, Writing, Mathematics, Science, History, and Geography.* Final discussion draft.

Massachusetts Department of Education. March 1995. *English Language Arts Curriculum Content Chapter: Constructing and Conveying Meaning.* Draft.

Michigan State Board of Education. September 1994. *Core Curriculum Content Standards and Benchmarks for Academic Content Standards for English Language Arts.* Draft.

New York State Education Department. October 1994. *Curriculum, Instruction, and Assessment: Preliminary Draft Framework for English Language Arts.*

North Carolina Department of Public Instruction. 1992. *Competency-Based Curriculum. Teacher Handbook: Communication Skills, K–12.*

North Dakota Department of Public Instruction. 1994. *English Language Arts Curriculum Frameworks: Standards and Benchmarks.*

South Carolina English Language Arts Curriculum Framework Writing Team. February 1995. *English Language Arts Framework.* Field review draft.

1

EMPHASIS: OVERVIEW OF COMPONENTS, EXPLORING CHARACTER

RESPONDING TO LITERARY ELEMENTS

Through Dialogue Journals and Minilessons

When the kids in my sixth-grade class are reading, so am I. That book often becomes the subject of a book talk. It doesn't take long for kids to start asking "How's your book?" in their letters to me. I always respond honestly, as in the following letter:

Dear Emily,

Right now I'm reading *The Facts and Fictions of Minna Pratt* by Patricia MacLachlan (1988). The techniques of characterization in this novel are superb. It has just the right balance of telling and revealing character traits. Minna is a very unique and yet very ordinary teenager. Her mother is a writer and never asks her any ordinary mother questions. Minna hates this. Also she is experiencing love for the first time. It happens while she's playing *Mozart* on the cello. His name is Lucas and his family is normal. At least that's the way Minna sees it at present. I have a feeling things may change. MacLachlan has written this in the present tense so it reads as if it is happening at the very moment that I'm reading it! Thanks for asking.

Ms. D

We read for sustained chunks of time in class and choose our own books from a variety of sources: classroom, school, public, and personal libraries. Students are required to write at least one letter per week in a reading dialogue journal. Every class begins with a five-minute minilesson, during which I focus on the strategies mature readers use, present book and author talks, and model my own responses to the adolescent novels I read (Atwell, 1987). My classroom library contains more than 600 paperbacks chosen especially for adolescent readers and includes novels, poetry, short story collections, and nonfiction material.

Early in the year, I give a series of book talks about adolescent novels I have read and loved. I read a carefully chosen excerpt that is sure to grab readers' interest, and I model my own responses to the book. In book talks, I've mentioned my understanding of Jody's anger, confusion and unending pain in *The Year without Michael* by Susan Beth Pfeffer (1988), my empathy for Louise in Katherine Paterson's *Jacob Have I Loved* (1988), and my awe at the beauty of Natalie Babbitt's language in *Tuck Everlasting* (1985).

The realization that I find value in adolescent novels gives kids the validation they need for their own feelings about these books. Being a member of the community of readers in my classroom stemmed from my increasing familiarity with, and respect for, adolescent literature. I began reading adolescent novels in order to be able to recommend books to kids, but my response to these novels took me by surprise. The more I read, the more I wanted to read. As a result, I've discovered a plethora of quality literature written expressly for teenagers, and I have been compelled to share my enthusiasm for these books with my kids. As Nancie Atwell (1987) says, "Living the literature becomes possible for students when teachers live the literature, too" (p. 200).

When kids begin to choose books that I've mentioned in book talks, I focus minilessons on the things I notice in the literature: author's use of setting, characterization, theme, conflict, use of language, and the relationship of the author's ideas to my world. I use adolescent literature I have read to illustrate these points.

SETTING

Julie of the Wolves by Jean Craighead George (1972) exemplifies the different ways in which an author might use setting in a novel. George's vivid description of the Alaskan tundra pulls readers into the story, making them feel as if they are there. She also uses setting to signal changes in action, to manipulate the reader's feelings, and to express ideas. Since *Julie of the Wolves* is a survival story, the setting also affects the actions and reactions of the character. I discuss these uses of setting in separate minilessons and always illustrate by reading a passage.

The connection between the character and the setting is evident in many passages from this novel. George uses the setting to emphasize the character's feelings in the following passage:

> The wind, the empty sky, the deserted earth—Miyax had felt the bleakness of being left behind once before.

She could not remember her mother very well, for Miyax was scarcely four when she died, but she did remember the day of her death. The wind was screaming wild high notes and hurling ice-filled waves against the beach, Kapugen was holding her hand and they were walking. When she stumbled, he put her on his shoulders, and high above the beach she saw thousands of birds diving toward the sea. The jaegers screamed and the sandpipers cried. The feathered horns of the comical puffins dropped low, and Kapugen told her they seemed to be grieving with him. (p. 75)

I ask students how this scene looks in their minds' eyes, how it makes them feel, and how they think Miyax and Kapugen are feeling. I allow them to respond, to agree, and to disagree with one another. In this exchange, all ideas are respected and none are deemed wrong. The suggestion of a parallel between the barrenness of the scene and the sorrow and loneliness of the characters emerges from this sharing. I conclude the discussion by suggesting that they try to notice the ways authors use setting in the novels they are reading.

Near the end of class, I bring the kids together and invite them to share anything they have noticed about the minilesson topic in their books. During one week-long discussion of setting, students shared what they noticed about the settings in the books they were reading. Bobby commented, "In Hatchet, the way the author describes the place makes me feel as scared and cold as Brian." Janet, who was reading *Julie of the Wolves*, remarked, "I found another place where Jean George makes me feel warm inside just like Miyax feels. It says about Kapugen's little house: 'It was rosy-gray on the outside. Inside, it was gold-brown.' That feels warm and safe." The wonder in their voices impressed me more than their words. They seemed surprised to have made such discoveries in their reading. What's more, others chose to read those books the very next day.

A few weeks later I received the following journal letter:

Dear Ms. D,

I'm reading *Snow Bound* by Harry Mazer. I remembered what we said in the minilessons a few weeks ago, the setting ones. I think Harry Mazer did some of those things too. In one part Tony is walking away from the car. He is just like a speck in the white snow walking and walking. The way Mazer wrote it I can see Tony in my mind. It makes me feel like he's so alone and will probably die. I think Tony feels like that too. And Cindy too because she sees him from the car window.

Ken

I doubt that Ken will ever forget that authors can use settings to manipulate readers' feelings and responses.

Allowing kids to select their own books, and to respond to them personally, provides them with a safe way to explore literary elements without fear of being wrong. In my response, I reinforced the kind of exploration Ken was doing:

Dear Ken,

Mazer sure does use setting in *Snow Bound* in many of the ways that we saw Jean George use setting in *Julie of the Wolves*. The example you used in your letter is great. It illustrates an author using setting to make the reader feel a certain way. The picture of Tony getting smaller and smaller as he walked up the snow-covered hill made me feel hopeless too. It made me think that the chances of their surviving were next to impossible. You made a good point. Thanks for sharing it with me.

Ms. D.

THEME

As a junior high student, I found theme difficult to identify in literature. As a result, I was utterly amazed at the ease with which my students began to note the universal ideas and feelings behind the stories they were reading and to connect those stories with their own lives. The following journal letters illustrate how the students talked about theme.

Dear Ms. D,

I just finished *The Friendship* and *The Gold Cadillac* but in this letter I will be zeroing on *The Friendship*. I've seen something in *The Friendship* that I think has something to do with peer pressure. When Tom Bee saved the white shopkeeper's life, he said he can call him by his first name, but now he changed his mind because the other white men said that it was bad that he was letting a black man call him by his first name so he backed out of the deal. He didn't do what was right and he listened to others even though he promised. What do you think?

Amy

Dear Ms. D,

In *Midnight Hour Encores* she was a very feeling person. Her love for her father was hidden in other things she did, like fighting and music.

He [Bruce Brooks] was saying love comes in many different ways, not just hugging and kissing.

I finished *The Shadow Club*. It was so full of hate for certain people, it burned.

Kay

My response to letters such as these is crucial, for it is in my letters to students that I am able to prod each one a little further. Many times that prodding is affirmation for their ideas and explorations. It is human nature to continue taking a risk when you receive positive feedback for the ones you have already taken.

Dear Kay,

I must read *Midnight Hour Encores* now because of the theme, "love comes in many different ways." Most of us think hugging and kissing are the only expressions of love. The fact that this book points out other ways love can be expressed makes it an important novel.

Oh no! You always say things that make me have to read the book. *The Shadow Club* is a must now too. The ad in the Trumpet Club brochure is what made me buy the book for our library. Your remark, "It is so full of hate . . . it burns," should replace their ad! Would you do a book talk?

Ms. D

When I return to theme in later minilessons, I use books that students have suggested in journal letters and share times. This year's suggestions included *A Wrinkle in Time* by Madeleine L'Engle (1976), *Roll of Thunder, Hear My Cry* by Mildred D. Taylor (1981), and *The Outsiders* by S. E. Hinton (1982, 1967). These suggestions change from class to class and from year to year. That fact alone suggests the richness of allowing students to freely explore the literary value of the books they choose to read.

CONFLICT

In discussing conflict, I always choose a novel that has a combination of internal and external conflicts. This year I used *The Island Keeper* by Harry Mazer (1981) because a student had recently done a book talk about it. Conflict always creates lively share time discussions and detailed journal letters. Perhaps the turmoil of adolescence makes it easy for these readers to identify with both external and internal conflict, especially in novels that have teenage characters. These letters, written by students of varying abilities, each exhibit a very real understanding of conflict.

> Dear Ms. D,
>
> I am still reading *Let the Circle Be Unbroken*. In it I like the way Mildred Taylor shows the inner conflict of Stacey, like when he walks off into the woods or when Cassie asks him questions. I think one of Mildred Taylor's inspiring authors was Mark Twain because it's kind of about the same topic and the style of writing are similar. I can understand how Stacey feels with a girl he likes getting pregnant with a white man, and learning about being a man and all the troubles you have to face, and doing it without Papa there. It would be hard.

> Dennis

Dennis focuses on more than one conflict in Taylor's novel, but he doesn't stop there. He goes on to compare Taylor and Twain! Is this simply reading or is it literature study? I say it's both. Dennis's sophisticated response to this book indicates real involvement as a reader. He is doing much more than a surface reading. In the next letter, Anne's response goes beyond a single book. She has begun to group books by theme and conflict.

> Dear Ms. D,
>
> At the beginning of the year I read *The Twin Connection*. It wasn't a great book but it relates to *Pen Pals, Rumble Fish, The Makeover Summer,* and *Just As Long As We're Together.* All these books are by different authors but the type of conflict is the same. JELOUSEY is the most popular area of conflict in my book because people of different ages can take part in feeling the same way. Jelousey can be an interesting area of conflict if you look at it with the right conclusion. Sometimes the jelousey is open and jumps from the page to your mind like in the *Twin Connection, Pen Pals, The Makeover Summer,* and *Just As Long As We're Together,* and sometimes it's hidden in the character's heart like *Rumble Fish* where you have to read between the lines to find it. I like these types of books.

> Anne

Again, my response reinforces the risk Anne took with her thinking about books and conflicts:

Dear Anne,

You're really thinking. Noticing how conflicts are repeated in a number of books and seeing how the same conflict is treated differently in those books is exactly the kind of thinking I'd hoped you would do this year. Keep it up.

Ms. D

The more literary elements I highlight in minilessons and the more I share my responses to adolescent novels, the more kids talk about their books in those terms. The mutual honesty that grows from shared interests, shared respect, and a common ground of literature is at the heart of my students' willingness to take risks in their responses to books. Before I had even addressed the idea of symbolism in a minilesson, Eric brought it up in his letter.

Dear Ms. D,

I just finished *The Dollar Man*. I loved it. I really liked the ending when he left the money and the watch behind on the bus seat. I guess that was to show he was leaving his father behind him.

Eric

I asked Eric to read this letter during the next day's share session. One student added, "I didn't think of that, but now I see what you mean. Keeping the watch and the dollar was a way of keeping his father in his life but it didn't help him at all." A debate about this symbolism resulted in kids bringing up other books. John said,

In *Rumble Fish*, when Motorcycle Boy broke into the pet store, took the fighting fish, and brought them to the water to be set free, it signified the rage inside of him being let out. He didn't express himself violently like I expected. Instead, his actions alone were symbols of his feelings.

The learning that grew out of this sharing of ideas among students can't be equaled in any other atmosphere. It is a forceful reminder that student sharing is a powerful instructional tool. With Eric's permission, I used his letter to introduce symbolism to my other classes.

In the final journal letter of the year, I ask students to write to me about how they had changed as readers and about their feelings about books and reading workshop. Their letters are always revealing:

When I came here I thought of reading as a bunch of words on paper that you just read. Now after minilessons and share times, I see that reading is an experience. I am now able to find the true meaning of a book. Minilessons taught me about books and their meanings. The one that influenced me most was the one where you talked about the universal message of a book. This taught me to look beyond the words on the page and see what they really meant.

Share times helped me to see the changes that were happening to me by sharing the things I had noticed in my reading that day.

The reason I have changed from a plain old reader to a reader that looks farther than the cover of the book is the journal.

I used to think good literature was a book with a good plot, but now I judge a good book by its characters.

At first I was embarrassed to share my ideas or to give my opinion on a certain book. But now I've learned that your opinion on a book can't be wrong.

There is magic in our classrooms when kids discover their own ideas. It happens because of the atmosphere we create, because of our enthusiasm for literature, and because kids have the freedom to choose their own books and to have their own ideas without fear of being wrong. But most of all it happens because we respect kids and their ideas and insist on the same from them. We are equals in the world of literature. A mutual honesty permeates our written and oral talk about books and the ideas they spark in us. This atmosphere is safe. It supports taking risks as readers and as thinkers. It validates each individual's ideas and promotes the exploration of new ones. This atmosphere allows for the transaction between the text and the reader that creates what Rosenblatt (1978) calls the poem, the meaning, and the merit of the literary experience. It creates a place where books become literature in the minds and hearts of adolescents.

REFERENCES

Atwell, N. (1987) . *In the Middle: Reading, Writing, and Learning with Adolescents.* Portsmouth, NH: Boynton/Cook.

Rosenblatt, L. (1978). *The Reader, the Text, the Poem: The Transactional Theory of the Literary Work.* Carbondale Southern Illinois University Press.

ADOLESCENT LITERATURE CITED

Babbitt, N. (1985). *Tuck Everlasting.* New York: Farrar, Straus, & Giroux.

Blume, J. (1988). *Just as Long as We're Together.* New York: Dell.

Brooks, B. (1988). *Midnight Hour Encores.* New York: Harper Junior Books.

George, J. C. (1972). *Julie of the Wolves.* New York: Harper Junior Books.

Hinton, S. E. (1982, 1967). *The Outsiders.* New York: Dell.

_____. (1983, 1975). *Rumblefish.* New York: Dell.

L'Engle, M. (1976). *A Wrinkle in Time.* New York: Dell.

MacLachlan, P. (1988). *The Facts and Fictions of Minna Pratt.* New York: Harper Junior Books.

Mazer, H. (1974). *The Dollar Man.* New York: Dell.

_____. (1975). *Snow Bound.* New York: Dell.

_____. (1981). *The Island Keeper.* New York: Dell.

Pascal, F. (Creator). (1990). *Sweet Valley Twins: The Twin Connection.* New York: Bantam.

Paterson, K. (1990). *Jacob Have I Loved.* New York: Harper Trophy.

Paulsen, G. (1988). *Hatchet.* New York: Penguin USA

Pfeffer, S. B. (1988). *The Year without Michael.* New York: Bantam.

Shusterman, N. (1990). *The Shadow Club.* New York: Dell.

Taylor, M. D. (1987). *The Friendship and the Gold Cadillac.* New York: Dell.

_____. (1983). *Let the Circle Be Unbroken.* New York: Bantam.

_____. (1981). *Roll of Thunder, Hear My Cry.* New York: Bantam.

Weyn, S. (1988). *The Makeover Summer.* New York: Avon.

Wyeth, S. D. (1989). *PenPals.* New York: Dell.

Marie Dionisio, Louis M. Klein Middle School, Harrison, New York

| SPTC

I find the following four projects successful ways to deal with the concepts of setting, plot, theme, and characterization in short fiction. These projects follow my presentation and discussion of a particular short story, and so I feel that students are fairly ready to work with these concepts on their own.

I begin by dividing the class into groups of four. Each group chooses a short story of interest to its group and one that lends itself to the concepts under consideration. I enjoy this opener because it requires students to peruse and discuss a variety of stories.

Project one: setting. Each group creates a mural to represent the setting of the story it selected. Prior to working on the mural, the group submits a planning diagram and a one-page explanation of how setting influenced the outcome (or another aspect) of the story.

Project two: plot. Each group reviews its short story and converts the plot into a workable dialogue for a skit or puppet show. Each group then presents its dramatic version of the short story to the class, complete with costumes, props, sound effects, and other theatrical trappings.

Project three: theme. Each group prepares—with justifications—a thematic statement for its story. Members of the group then select a poem with a similar theme and present both story and poem to the class, explaining and justifying their thematic interpretation of both. Other students are expected to ask questions in preparation for a quiz on the material covered in this unit.

Project four: characterization. Each individual in a group selects one character from the group's short story. Putting themselves in the position of that character, they describe how they felt and why they acted as they did. They give their impressions of how other characters feel about them and tell what they think of other characters.

To conclude the unit, students complete a quiz on the concepts of setting, plot, theme, and characterization and on the specific literature covered in class. The total time works out to a hectic but interesting four weeks.

Don Snow, F. R. Haythorne Junior High School, Sherwood Park, Alberta, Canada

WORKING UP TO CHARACTER SKETCHES

Each quarter, students in my sophomore honors English classes are required to choose and read independently a challenging book in addition to the assigned literature readings. To help them prepare to write a character sketch in class as one of the quarterly assignments, students are given the following notetaking sheet several weeks in advance of the assignment:

Title of Book: _____

Name of Author: _____

Name of Character: _____

1. What did the writer reveal about the character through the following means? List examples for each.

    reactions of other characters:
    physical appearance and surroundings:
    speech:
    actions:
    direct statements:
    thoughts:

2. List as many appropriate adjectives as you can think of to describe the character.
3. List the single most dominant quality of the character. (Or, if two qualities seem equally important, list both.)
    List actions and statements from the book that illustrate this (these) characteristic(s).
4. Bring this sheet to class on the following date: _____.
    Be prepared to write a character sketch in class.

On the day of the assigned writing, the students bring their notes to class and are given the following assignment:

Based on the book that you read, write a character sketch that emphasizes one or two qualities of a character you have chosen. In the opening paragraph, identify the book and the character and state the thesis of the essay. Then, using examples from the book, write several paragraphs to support the thesis. Keep in mind that your final product should be a fluid description of the character and not simply a list of details. Finally, use the concluding paragraph to sum up the essay.

Having already identified one or two characteristics on which to focus and having listed specific examples from the book, the students are better able to organize their ideas and to write effective character sketches. The notetaking sheets yield concrete results in the students' final work.

Mary Ann Shaw, Rock Bridge High School, Columbia, Missouri

A RECOMMENDATION FOR TOM SAWYER

My seventh-grade class had just finished reading Twain's *Adventures of Tom Sawyer.* They had fallen in love with Tom, and they had enjoyed everything about the book. But now it was time for a test. Tom could turn anything into fun—why couldn't I make a test about him fun, too?

Instead of a conventional test, I presented each student with a recommendation form for the Marksam Boarding School. I told the class that Tom had applied and needed their references. I instructed students to use everything they had learned about Tom in their reading, to be honest and frank, generous where possible, and to describe any improvement the applicant had shown throughout the year (i. e., throughout the book).

The recommendation form, shown with abbreviated samples of student responses, can be easily adapted to many books about adolescents. It can be given as a test or creative writing assignment. Change the form to suit the book. Make it into a recommendation for college or a job. If I had used the idea for *A Separate Peace,* I would have included the category "Athletic Ability." An interesting variation would be to have each student write his or her recommendation from the specific viewpoint of just one other character in the book, thus getting greatly differing opinions from different students.

RECOMMENDATION FORM
THE MARKSAM BOARDING SCHOOL

The following student has applied for admission to the Marksam Boarding School: *Thomas Sawyer*

Your name has been submitted to the Admissions Committee as someone with extensive knowledge about the above-named candidate. We would appreciate your completing the following Recommendation Form as candidly as possible. Any detailed information you can provide us with regarding the applicant's academic record and personal qualifications would be most helpful.

Candidate's Name: Thomas Sawyer   *Age:* Around 12
Name of Parent or Guardian: Aunt Polly   *Sex:* M
Address, City: St. Petersburg   *State:* Missouri
Attendance Record: Very poor. Tom plays hooky often and would rather go swimming or fishing than attend school.
Physical Appearance: Tom is an appealing-looking child. However, his appearance would improve if he washed more frequently and wore shoes.

Academic Record

Attentiveness in Class: Tom has trouble concentrating in class. Recently he has been preoccupied with a young girl in class named Becky Thatcher. He sometimes finds his bug collection of more interest than his schoolwork.

Intellectual Ability: Tom is extremely clever and bright. Although he cannot memorize a thing for recitation, when he puts his mind to it he can learn anything. For example, he can quote many pages verbatim from his favorite pirate stories.

English (spelling, language usage, favorite books, etc.): Tom speaks English poorly. For example, he is always saying, "I'll learn you this." His writing and spelling are weak. Tom's favorite books are *Treasure Island* and *The Adventures of Robin Hood.*

Science (Describe applicant's understanding of the scientfic method): Tom knows a good deal about wildlife and is an expert on bugs. However, he has a poor understanding of the scientific method and he is very superstitious. He thought warts could be cured by throwing a dead cat over your shoulder in a graveyard.

Religious Instruction: Tom attends church and Sunday school regularly. He is eager to succeed and even managed to "win" a Bible, although it was later discovered the trophy was undeserved.

Character and Personality Evaluation

Peer Relationships (How does Tom interact with classmates and friends?): Tom is well-liked and admired for his daring, pluck, and cleverness. His best friends are Huck Finn (the town outcast) and Joe Harper. Tom gets along less well with boys from socially established families, whom he tends to antagonize.

Leadership Potential: Tom is a born leader. He even got his friends to paint a fence for him on a Saturday!

Perseverance: When Tom wants something he sticks to the task. It was through his single-minded determination that he and Huck found the treasure they were seeking.

Concern for Others: Tom used to be quite callous about other people's feelings. His Aunt Polly, especially, suffered because of his many thoughtless pranks. But lately, Tom has changed. His conscience got the better of him during Muff Potter's trial, and Tom even risked his own life in order to save Muff's. Tom's love of a young girl in town has also brought out his truly generous nature.

Other Comments (Please give us your overall assessment of the potential of this candidate): While it is true that Tom has been a poor student, he is obviously extremely bright and has potential. He has changed a lot over this year. While earlier he identified with the outcasts of the town, since he has discovered the buried treasure, won Becky Thatcher's love and the admiration of the town, he is very eager to become a respectable citizen. Judge Thatcher has taken a kindly interest in Tom, is investing the boy's money wisely for him, and has high hopes that Tom will become a lawyer. All this leads me to feel that Tom will do better at Marksam than he ever did in the St. Petersburg grade school. He is an enjoyable boy if you have a sense of humor and some patience, and he deserves a chance to prove himself at your school.

Signature: _____   Date: _____

By putting fictional characters in real-life situations, this assignment brings literature closer to home. It encourages students to think about what someone would write about them on a school or job application. It facilitates discussion on some interesting questions, such as "How do we judge character?" and "What are some other real-life situations in which it is important to make sound deductions about peoples' values?" Finally, students are better able to see that by analyzing fictional characters, we are better prepared to "read" real people, including ourselves.

Joan Brodsky Schur, Village School, New York, New York

CHARACTERIZATION THROUGH DIALOGUE

An important aspect of the study of the short story is characterization. But as Robert Probst has pointed out, study of literary concepts must take students' responsibilities into account. After the discussion of stories that emphasize character, I ask students to give their reaction to a certain character. After discussing the reactions, students are asked to find passages in the story that caused them to react the way they did. The passages cited will usually include all methods of characterization used by authors: the character's speech, thoughts, actions, appearance, and evidence of other characters' feelings toward this character.

When discussing a character's speech, students are first asked to pick specific words from the dialogue that helped form their impression of that character. They are directed to consider the content of the dialogue as well as the word choice and vocabulary of the character.

Next, students are divided into small groups. Each group then represents a character who has been studied recently. Each group is given several sentences to rewrite as dialogue as it would be spoken by their character. Some of the sentences are then shared with the rest of the class. Students hear how an idea expressed by Romeo would differ greatly from that same idea when spoken by Walter Mitty, for example.

Following this activity, students are assigned to write a conversation between any two characters of their choice. The characters can be real or fictional, but must be familiar to the class. Students enjoy matching unusual pairs and imagining the conversation they might have. The emphasis of the writing is on revealing character through speech, so careful attention is to be given to word choice and vocabulary. After the rough drafts are written, they are shared and discussed in writing groups.

Before revised copies are written, I review the punctuation rules regarding the use of quotation marks with dialogue. Students then rewrite and read their conversations to the entire class. Evaluation of the final writing follows with emphasis placed on the development of character through speech and the correct use of quotation marks.

Barbara A. Dressler, Cadott Community Schools, Cadott, Wisconsin

❘ ME TARZAN, YOU JANE

The two most common methods of studying a literary text in English class are talking and writing *about* it. A third alternative, one that is equally valuable but sometimes overlooked, asks students to explore the lives of the characters outside the perimeters of the story. The following three exercises will facilitate the active entry into a character's fictional world. They generally work better in the second half of the school year, when students are comfortable with the teacher and one another. A bit of previous work with creative dramatics in class helps as well.

1. Each student takes responsibility for one character in a story or novel. It's perfectly all right if several people work with the same character since duplication provides interesting opportunities for comparison and contrast. And don't overlook minor and even very minor characters when assignments are made. Based on what is revealed in the story (What does Daisy say about herself? What do others say about her? What does the narrator tell us about her past?) and what can be inferred (What does her behavior suggest about her personality?), the student writes an autobiography of that character. Encourage students to exercise creativity in imagining what the lives of characters might have been like before and after, as well as during the story. Autobiographies should be written in the voice of the character and should try to express as much of his or her personality as possible—not only biographical data, but likes, dislikes, feelings about self and about other characters in the story.

    At least two uses can be made of these autobiographies. Students can, of course, read all or parts of their work aloud, assuming the voices of the characters they wrote about. Another possibility is a talk show in which one student plays the moderator and others become celebrity guests by taking on the roles of the characters about whom they wrote. The moderator is responsible for compiling a list of interview questions that allow guests to talk about their lives and about their perceptions of the story of which they are a part. Although characters can be interviewed individually, a panel discussion is usually more fun because it leads to debate between characters about what's really happening in the story.

2. Divide the class into groups, assigning each group a character from a story or novel. After discussing this character's personality, interaction with other characters, and role in the story, the group rewrites the story (or selected scenes) as it might have been told from that character's point of view. Each group presents this version of the story to the class, through a group reading in which dialogue and narration have been parceled out or (ideally) as a skit. The class will be fascinated to discover how the tone, characterization, and sometimes even the basic plot of the story change as each group presents events from another character's point of view.

3. This final exercise can be done by the class as a whole, but small groups often generate more unusual scripts. Each group chooses a character from a particular story, writes (or improvises) new scenes for that character, and acts out these scenes before the class. These scenes can present events that took place before or after the story, such as a reformed Ebenezer Scrooge having Christmas dinner with the Cratchit family. Characters can also be placed in an entirely new situation—at a political rally or a party, on a storm-tossed ship, at the site of a murder. A third option is to take characters from several stories and bring them together in a new script. In each case, the object is to achieve a greater understanding of the psychological and intellectual complexities of fictional characters.

Paula Gray, Parkland Community College, Champaign, Illinois

CAREERS FOR CHARACTERS

As a response to the current emphasis on career skills, each of my eighth-grade students becomes a character in a novel or short story he or she has read and finds a job for that character. In the process students read fictional works, use media center resources, read and interpret classified ads, and write and type business letters and resumes. To spark their interest, I lead a class brainstorming session for details to include in a model resume and business letter, based on a character in a work we have read, for example Lillian Wright from Asimov's "Rain, Rain, Go Away." Using our ideas, I type these two documents in the appropriate format and distribute copies to the class. (See examples on page 22.)

Next, students choose a character from a self-selected novel or short story and list the character's talents, interests, and possible hobbies. They identify possible career choices for their characters by consulting media center sources such as the *Worker Trait Group Guide, Chronicle Guidance Occupational Library, Career Discovery Encyclopedia, OCCU-FACTS,* etc. There's a built-in artificiality to the process, but that often adds humor and flair to the assignment!

After identifying possible character careers, students investigate the classified sections of local newspapers in order to select possible job prospects for their characters. The students cut out the ads and rewrite them in sentence form, spelling out any abbreviations.

In the next step, each student writes a letter of application from the character to the company offering the job. This letter follows a business letter format and can be typed in the school's computer center. Students use our model letter of application for reference.

Finally, the student completes a resume for the character. Any names, dates, or places must be connected to the plot or the setting of the literary piece. Some students can benefit from a blank resume format developed in class.

This project helps students to integrate various resources such as the fictional source, the media center, a personal computer, and the newspaper.

Adaptations of the project could make it appropriate for both older and younger students. And, of course, although the career research in this project applies to a fictional character, students can use the same information to investigate personal career choices.

Shelley Mattson Gahn, Liberty Middle School, West Chester, Ohio

Careers for Characters

Sample Documents for "Rain, Rain, Go Away" by Isaac Asimov
APPLICATION LETTER

521 Stargazer Avenue
Outer Limits, Ohio 45012
July 30, 2010

Mr. William Jones, President
Jones Detective Agency
7411 Murphy Park Road
Outer Limits, Ohio 45012

Dear Mr. Jones:

   I am interested in the position of assistant detective which you advertised for recently in the *Sugar-Coated Times*. For the past two years I have been keeping careful surveillance of my neighbors, Mr. and Mrs. Sakkaro. The mysterious disappearance of the Sakkaro family is not a mystery to me because of my close observation of their unusual habits. My experience with my neighbors has made me aware of my talent for undercover work.

   The enclosed résumé will give you more details of my background. I would like to use my experience for the Jones Detective Agency. I would appreciate the opportunity of meeting you.

   I am available for an interview at your convenience.

Sincerely yours,

Lillian Wright

Some Key Aspects of Application Letters

1. Begin your letter with a positive statement about your job skills.
2. Include the position you are applying for.
3. Include how you heard of the position.
4. Explain why you are interested, and that you have included a résumé.
5. Let the employer know that you are available for an interview.
6. Review business letter format, if necessary.

- -

RÉSUMÉ
Lillian Wright

ADDRESS:	521 Stargazer Avenue Outer Limits, Ohio 45012
TELEPHONE:	(461) 247-3313
EMPLOYMENT GOAL:	I would like to work for a detective agency.
PERSONAL:	Date of Birth: October 1, 1977 Place of Birth: Spaced Out, Ohio Health: Good Social Security Number: 211-11-1111
EDUCATION: 1991–1995	Outer Limits High School 333 Alien Avenue, Outer Limits, Ohio 45012
INTERESTS:	Star gazing, washing windows, and people watching
WORK EXPERIENCE: 1995–1998	Dieting for a Sugar-free Life 820 Sweetness Street, Outer Limits, Ohio 45012, (461) 222-2121 Duties: Advisor
REFERENCES:	Mr. Sakkaro, Expert Stargazer, 522 Stargazer Avenue, Outer Limits, Ohio 45012, (461) 222-2323 Mr. George Wright, Couch Potato, 521 Stargazer Avenue, Outer Limits, Ohio 45012, (461) 247-3313

Résumé Reminders

1. No abbreviations.
2. Include at least one work experience.
3. Include at least two references.
4. Include dates for the education and work experience sections.
5. Write the book title and the author's name at the top of your character's résumé.

Note: In some cases, information won't be included in the story. You can infer information such as work experience and education, but be prepared to explain your choices.

ANOTHER ANGLE FOR BOOK REPORTS

For a departure from the typical written book report, my students and I recommend this idea. Students select and focus on one significant character from a book read in class. Then from their knowledge of the plot and their understanding of the chosen character, students select newspaper articles that they believe would interest the character. Some examples are listed below.

- news items the character would read
- cartoons the character would enjoy
- types of entertainment the character would choose to attend
- special columns or sections that would interest the character (advice column, book reviews, sports, stock market, obituaries)
- advertised consumer items the character might need or like to have (clothing, food, appliances, vehicles)
- particular classified ads that would appeal to the character (personal ads, garage sales, help wanted, pets for sale)

Students decide on appropriate articles, clip them out, mount them on separate sheets of paper, and write brief explanations underneath.

This book report technique is also suitable for group work. After several students have read the same book, they meet together to select articles and ads from the newspaper. After deciding which are the most appropriate, students clip out their selections and construct a poster labeled with the name of their character. Each completed poster can be explained to the class by a member of the group, and a wall of the classroom can be devoted to a display.

Brenda J. Clark, Spring, Texas

2 | EMPHASIS: THEME

STORYBOARD POTPOURRI

I'm not sure of the origin of the storyboard, but I have successfully used variations on it in my classroom for a number of years.

The most obvious use of the storyboard is that of a summary tool. The storyboard represents the student's own interpretation of the key events in the work.

For this use, my procedure is as follows: after students read a short story, novel, or poem, or watch a movie, I distribute blank "storyboards"—sheets of paper divided into six equal frames. I ask students to fill in the six blocks with pictures representing the six key scenes in the work. These can be represented in any form from stick figures to elaborate drawings. Beneath each drawing the student writes a short sentence or phrase describing what is represented by the drawing. These storyboards can then be discussed with the class and displayed.

But the storyboard can be used to enhance understanding in other ways as well:

1. Students may expand the short sentences or phrases in each box into a written summary of the work.
2. Students may meet in small groups to explain and defend their storyboard interpretations of a work. I have found it rare for two students to have similar storyboards, except possibly for the first and last frames, so small group discussion can give students practice in expressing themselves as well as exposure to a variety of possible interpretations of a work.
3. The storyboards can be used as "teasers" to encourage recreational reading. Instead of a standard book report, a student fills out the storyboard on the book, *up to the main conflict*. When displayed in the classroom or library, these previews pique students' curiosity and may persuade them to read the book to find out how the conflict was resolved.
4. To provide practice in sequencing, storyboards may be cut apart and their frames shuffled. Students may then work individually or in pairs or small groups to arrange the frames in a sensible sequence. In some cases, one sequence will be clearly the most logical, but in other

cases, students may be able to justify more than one sequence for the frames. Thus, this task can involve critical thinking and discussion of cause and effect and of what factors create a logical progression.

5. Storyboards might also be used as an alternate to journal entries. Students might be asked to depict in storyboard frames the major events of their weekend or vacation. In this variation, students must select events to portray and decide which details or actions will best convey the events. When the storyboards are completed, peer feedback makes it clear if the student's story has been understood.

John Powers, Magnolia High School, Anaheim, California

BUT WHAT IS THE STORY REALLY ABOUT?

When students have finished reading a short story and I ask them, "What is the story about?" they invariably respond with plot summaries. So I have devised a way to use these plot summaries to focus attention on theme.

I start by writing the heading *Themes* on the chalkboard or overhead projector. Then I ask several students in turn to answer the question "What is the story about?" and to fill in any important points that the others might have left out. As students answer, I extract general concepts from their answers and list these concepts on the chalkboard or overhead projector under *Themes*. For instance, if a student says that the main character in the novel can't decide whether or not to marry, I list *Marriage* in the column. If a student mentions that one character becomes ill or dies, I write down *Illness* or *Death*.

Next, I ask students, "What does the author seem to think or say on this subject?" as I point in turn to each of the items listed under *Themes*. Students respond with their impressions of the author's views and, if possible, with support for their opinions. For instance, if I ask, "What does the author think about death?" I might expect a student to say, "The author thinks that death is something that you can overcome if you refuse to be afraid" and to cite a dialogue among several characters where this view prevails. As students respond, I jot down their phrases and sentences next to the appropriate concept listed on the chalkboard. Looking over the final list of phrases and sentences, students should be able to judge which topics represent major themes of the work by the amount of information they were able to supply.

The process of moving from particular events in a work to theme statements helps students understand how a writer develops theme through plot. And if the list that students dictate is expanded to include examples of imagery, character development, and style, the completed outline then illustrates the ties between events of the plot and other elements of the work.

Arlene Pullen, Carteret High School, Carteret, New Jersey

DEALING WITH STEREOTYPES
In a Topical Unit

The activity below, reprinted from William Nagy's Teaching Vocabulary to Improve Reading Comprehension *(NCTE/ERIC, 1988), can be used at the middle school level in a topical or thematic unit that includes works depicting aspects of urban and rural life or in the study of stereotypes.*

Divide the class into two groups, assigning a recorder for each group. The groups will each be brainstorming word associations. One group should brainstorm as many words or phrases as they can connected with the word *city*. The other group should brainstorm words or phrases connected with the phrase *small town*. The recorder in each group should write down the words and phrases brainstormed.

After giving the groups about three minutes for the brainstorming session, ask each recorder to read the group's list. Encourage students to ask questions about the words and allow them to express further ideas about the aptness of the words on their list. Then introduce the concept of *stereotype* to the students, explaining it in terms of oversimplified and formulaic views and attitudes about people, places, or institutions. Ask the students whether or not any of the items on their list reflected stereotypes of big cities or small towns and the people who live in them. Spend some time discussing stereotypes, noting that people and places do not often fit the stereotyped images used to describe them.

Deborah Little, Alabama State University, Montgomery

USING YOUNG ADULT PROBLEM FICTION AND NONFICTION
To Produce Critical Readers

We are English teachers, not guidance counselors." I have never forgotten these words said by my professor in a methods class. Nonetheless, it is difficult to ignore the many problems facing today's adolescents, especially when uncomfortable topics often arise as students engage in reader-response activities with literature. Students want to talk about their problems, but they often don't want everyone to know that they are the ones whose problems are being discussed. Students who are being sexually abused, for example, won't go to the library to check out books on the topic because they know that they will become suspect. Feeling that students would benefit from reading and discussing such books, I decided to devise a way that would enable students to discuss the issues concerning them in a way that was literary, not counselor-based.

SELECTING THE PROBLEMS

To begin the process, I ask students to identify all of the problems affecting adolescents, especially those that put them "at-risk" in today's schools. Students might generate a list of topics that resembles the following: abused children, adopted teens, AIDS, alcohol and drugs, alienation and identity, anorexia nervosa, children of divorce (or being raised by a single parent), children of poverty, death and dying, delinquency, handicapped youth, homosexuality, multicultural concerns/prejudice, stress and suicide, teenage pregnancy, and teenage sexuality. Because there will probably be too many topics on the resulting list for a single class to explore in any kind of depth, I ask the class to select five topics if the class has about 25 students, and I have students group themselves so that five students are in each group and each group is responsible for studying one topic. For this particular article, I have chosen the following five topics to illustrate the process: abused children, eating disorders, homosexuality, teenage pregnancy, and stress and suicide.

SELECTING THE BOOKS

I then give students a list of several annotated young adult novels and have them choose one to read with each member reading a different book that pertains to their particular topic. For additional annotations, there are many reputable sources such as *The ALAN Review* and NCTE's *Books for You, High Interest—Easy Reading*, and *Your Reading*. It is important to provide several choices for students and to select books that have different problem situations. As the following list of annotations reveals, various problems are associated with each broad category. Abuse, for example, takes many forms and is not limited to sexual abuse.

ANNOTATED LIST OF YOUNG ADULT NOVELS

Abused Children
- *Everything Is Not Enough* by Sandy Asher; Dell, 1987 (155 pp.). Michael's new job introduces him to Tricia, who is being abused by her boyfriend. (physical abuse by boyfriend)
- *A Different Kind of Love* by Michael Borich; Signet, 1987 (157 pp.). Weeble's uncle comes to live with her and her mother and makes sexual advances towards Weeble. (sexual abuse by uncle)
- *Chinese Handcuffs* by Chris Crutcher; Dell, 1991 (220 pp.). Jennifer, an all-star basketball player, seems to have everything going

for her, but no one knows she is being sexually abused by her stepfather. (sexual abuse by stepfather)

- *Abby, My Love* by Hadley Irwin; Atheneum, 1985 (146 pp.). Abby's father, a prominent dentist, has been sexually abusing her, which prevents her from allowing herself to be intimate with Chip. (sexual abuse by father)
- *Putting Heather Together Again* by Marilyn Levy; Ballantine, 1989 (136 pp.). Seventeen-year-old Heather suffers from a date rape and has difficulty telling anyone about it. (sexual abuse by boyfriend)
- *The Big Way Out* by Peter Silsbee; Dell, 1987 (180 pp.). Paul's father has manic depressive disorder and his abusive threats and violence have the family on guard all of the time. (physical abuse by father)

Eating Disorders

- *Second Star to the Right* by Deborah Hautzig; Greenwillow Books, 1981 (151 pp.). Leslie finds herself in a hospital for people with eating disorders and she tries to reconstruct how she got there.
- *Heads You Win, Tails I Lose* by Isabelle Holland; Dell, 1973 (158 pp.). Melissa is overweight and takes diet pills because she thinks being thin is the way to be popular and loved.
- *Early Disorder* by Rebecca Josephs; Farrar, Straus, and Giroux, 1980 (185 pp.). The only thing Willa can control is her diet, but even that gets out of control.
- *The Best Little Girl in the World* by Steven Levenkron; Warner Books, 1991 (253 pp.). Kessa thinks she's grossly overweight even though she is only five-foot-four and 98 pounds.
- *I Was a 15-Year-Old Blimp* by Patti Stren; Harper and Row, 1985 (185 pp.). Gabby starts taking laxatives and purging her meals in order to lose weight so she can capture the attention of a boy she likes.

Homosexuality

- *Happily Ever After* by Hila Colman; Scholastic, 1986 (156 pp.). Now that they've graduated from high school, Melanie is ready for marriage but Paul has other issues to address. (coming out—male)
- *Annie On My Mind* by Nancy Garden; Farrar, Straus, and Giroux, 1982 (233 pp.). Liza and Annie are drawn to each other at an art museum, and Liza

forces herself to stay away until she can no longer deny her feelings. (coming out—female)

- *The Drowning of Stephan Jones* by Bette Greene; Bantam, 1991 (217 pp.).
  Andy is incensed when two gay men move into town, and his homophobia leads to tragedy. (homophobia)
- *Jack* by A. M. Homes; Macmillan, 1989 (220 pp.).
  In the midst of dealing with his parents' divorce, Jack learns that his father is a homosexual. (dealing with a homosexual father)
- *Night Kites* by M.E. Kerr; Harper and Row, 1987 (216 pp.).
  During his senior year, Erick falls for his best friend's girlfriend and finds out that his brother is gay and has AIDS. (dealing with a homosexual brother who has AIDS)
- *Breaking Up: A Novel* by Norma Klein; Avon Books, 1982 (224 pp.).
  Not only are Alison's parents getting a divorce, but the cause is that her mother is involved with another woman. (dealing with a homosexual mother)
- *Rumors and Whispers* by Marilyn Levy; Fawcett Juniper, 1990 (153 pp.).
  Sarah offers her gay brother the loving support he needs after their parents throw him out of the house. (dealing with a homosexual brother)
- *Bad Boys* by Diana Wieler; Delacorte Press, 1992 (184 pp.). Although A. J.'s alias is "bad boy" for being so tough on his hockey team, his emotions are taxed when he learns that his best friend is gay. (dealing with a homosexual best friend)
- *I Never Got to Say Goodbye* by Alida E. Young; Willowisp Press, 1988 (175 pp.).
  Traci's uncle has AIDS; and, when his roommate dies of AIDS, she and her uncle attend help groups and decide to make Danny a panel for the AIDS Memorial Quilt. (dealing with a homosexual uncle with AIDS)

Teenage Pregnancy

- *Stranger, You and I* by Patricia Calvert; Charles Scribner's Sons, 1987 (152 pp.).
  Zee, a junior, gets pregnant after "one time" and her friend, Hugh, helps her decide what to do.
- *No More Saturday Nights* by Norma Klein; Fawcett Juniper, 1988 (264 pp.).
  When Tim's pregnant girlfriend tries to "sell" her baby, Tim decides to raise the baby himself during his freshman year at college.

- *That Night* by Alice McDermott; Farrar, Straus, and Giroux, 1987 (184 pp.).
  Because Sheryl is only 15 when she gets pregnant, her mother decides that she will give the baby up for adoption but never consults the father about his feelings.
- *Don't Look and It Won't Hurt* by Richard Peck; Avon Books, 1979 (173 pp.).
  Ellen becomes pregnant at 17 and struggles with the decision of whether or not to keep the baby.
- *Bird at the Window* by Jan Truss; Harper and Row, 1980 (215 pp.).
  Angela refuses to talk about her pregnancy and struggles with the decision to keep the baby or have an abortion.
- *If Not For You* by Margaret Willey; Harper and Row, 1988 (160 pp.).
  Bonnie's best friend's sister, Linda, drops out of school in order to marry Ray and have his baby, and Bonnie thinks that is so romantic until she does some babysitting for the couple.

Stress and Suicide

- *I Can Hear the Mourning Dove* by James Bennett; Houghton Mifflin, 1990 (224 pp.).
  After Grace's father's sudden death, she attempts suicide and spends most of her junior year in a mental institution.
- *Chinese Handcuffs* by Chris Crutcher; Dell, 1991 (220 pp.).
  Dillon struggles with his own life after witnessing his brother's suicide.
- *So Long at the Fair* by Hadley Irwin; McElderry, 1988 (202 pp.). Joel's best friend, Ashley, commits suicide, and Joel is left to accept his life without her in it.
- *Just for the Summer* by Karin N. Mango; Harper Collins, 1990 (204 pp.).
  Jenny befriends Rollo, who suffers from guilt because of his inability to prevent his father's suicide.
- *Blindfold* by Sandra McCuaig; Holiday House, 1990 (167 pp.).
  Fifteen-year-old Sally has to deal with the suicides of two brothers who were her best friends.
- *Because of Lissa* by Carolyn Meyer; Bantam Books, 1990 (192 pp.).
  After Lissa's suicide, four teenagers establish a hotline at their school for troubled students.
- *How Could You Do It, Diane?* by Stella Pevsner; Clarion Books, 1989 (183 pp.).
  Fourteen-year-old Bethany finds her well-loved, older stepsister's body after she commits suicide.

■ *Right Behind the Rain* by Joyce Sweeney; Delacorte Press, 1990 (160 pp.).
Carla's brother's suicide is prevented thanks to her.

USING READER-RESPONSE JOURNALS

I give students two weeks or so to read their individual novels, keeping a reading response journal while they read. Students should note their thoughts while they read and can be prompted by the following questions: What advice would you give the protagonist if he or she were your best friend? Comment each time any character reminds you of someone or something you have read or heard about. What were the events leading up to the protagonist's main problem? What were the telling signs that a character had a problem? Because of the intensity of the topics, it is important to warn students not to discuss in a careless manner the names or identities of people they know.

RESEARCHING NONFICTION MATERIALS

After students have finished reading their novels, I take them to the library and have them conduct research on their topics. Each student finds at least one reference and cites a minimum of ten facts pertaining to the subject. Additionally, students locate information on where a person with such a problem can go for help. I stress that sources and facts must be cited accurately. In this way, I present a mini-lesson on the MLA style or APA style of reporting research in a meaningful context.

After students individually find their facts, they reconvene in their groups so that each group has a minimum of 50 facts pertaining to the topic. I ask them to select the best 25 statements to be included in a class-generated fact sheet with corresponding information for finding help. By having students reject half of their information, I ensure that discussions about credibility of source, recency of information, relevancy of information, and the need to properly cite information will ensue. For example, consider these facts about teenage suicide:

1. Suicide is the third leading cause of death for 15- to 19-year-olds, and the rate for children under the age of 15 has increased almost 800% since 1950 (Stupple, 1987, p. 64).
2. Suicide is now the second leading cause of teenage deaths, topped only by vehicle fatalities (Edwards, 1988, p. 297).
3. According to the National Center for Health Statistics, about 5,000 young people commit suicide each year, and other research indicates

that another 500,000 others attempt to do so (Spoonhour, 1985, p. 76).

4. A federal survey of high school students by the national Centers for Disease Control (CDC) found that 27% "thought seriously"about killing themselves in the preceding year and 8% made actual attempts (*St. Petersburg Times*, 1991, p. 1A)

5. Over 1000 American teenagers attempt suicide each day, which translates into 57 attempts per hour; one teenager succeeds every hour and a half (Patros & Shamoo, 1989).

6. The suicide rate is highest in the spring, especially in the month of May (Leight, 1986, p. 143).

7. There are three irrefutable statements that can be made about teen suicide: 1) an attempt usually follows something shattering from a week to a month beforehand, 2) 80% of young people who try to or do commit suicide give some explicit warning of their unhappiness, and 3) 70% of attempts or actual suicides are made while under the influence of drugs or alcohol (Hallowell, 1987, p. 70).

8. Hopelessness is a better indicator than depression in assessing whether a person is likely to commit suicide (American Association of Suicidology, 1975).

There is an obvious contradiction, for example, between points one and two. Students might want to look at each article and decide who is the more credible source, might locate another source which corroborates one or the other, or might opt for point two since it is the more recent of the two. Points three, four, and five all deal with the number of suicides that occur in a specific time period. Students might discuss which statement is the most meaningful to them. If students must eliminate half of their facts, which would they omit from points six, seven, and eight? In any case, students have to use their critical thinking skills in order to determine which facts should be included.

USING NONFICTION INFORMATION IN LITERARY STUDY

After students become knowledgeable about the facts of their particular problem of study, I ask them to examine their respective young adult novels to see if the author did his or her homework regarding the portrayal of the character with the problem. In other words, is the problem presented accurately? Do the characters behave consistently with what is known to be true? Was the character stereotypical or was the information presented accurately in the context of the character's life? These questions should be discussed in their groups.

At this point, there are at least three group options that can be presented to students: 1) Students may write a literary analysis of one of the young adult novels using the information they gathered in their research as their guide; 2) students may write a short story depicting the characters as accurately and as three-dimensionally as possible; or 3) students may want to write a different scene or an alternative ending for one of the novels that is consistent with what they've learned to be true. Option three also allows students to incorporate the knowledge they acquired regarding where students can go for help if it is needed. People who are suicidal, for example, should contact a local Suicide Prevention Service, Stress Management Consultants, School Counseling Services, Suicide Crisis Centers, or the Suicide Hotline: these numbers are usually available in a phone book. Students (and sometimes teachers) often don't know about the help that is available.

CONCLUSION

There are several reasons why teachers should incorporate such a unit into their teaching. The topics are relevant and meaningful and provide students with opportunities to discuss such things in a fact-based rather than in an opinionated and emotional manner. Students conduct research that requires credible sources and accuracy of citations which allows teachers to conduct meaningful discussions about these research concerns. Students are able to apply information from nonfiction in their literary analyses of fictional material. Students are exposed to a myriad of young adult novels that they may want to read on their own after the unit's completion. And, perhaps most importantly, students become knowledgeable about how to find such information if it ever does become needed.

BIBLIOGRAPHY

American Association of Suicidology. *Suicide,* Summer, 1975.

Associated Press. "CDC: 1 in 12 Teens Try Suicide," *St. Petersburg Times,* September 20, 1991, p. lA ff.

Edwards, T. K "Providing Reasons for Wanting to Live," *Phi Delta Kappan,* December, 1988, p. 297 ff.

Gallo, D. R., (Chair) and the Committee on the Senior High Booklist. *Books for You: A Booklist for Senior High Students.* National Council of Teachers of English, 1985.

Hallowell, C. "Suicide: How to Save a Friend's Life," *YM,* October, 1987, p. 70 ff.

Leight, L. "Suicide: The Last Taboo," *New Woman,* May, 1986, p. 140 ff.

Matthews, D., (Chair) and the Committee to Revise *High Interest—Easy*

Reading. High Interest—Easy Reading for Junior and Senior High School Students. 5th ed. National Council of Teachers of English, 1988.

Nilsen, A. P. (Ed.), and the Committee on the Junior High and Middle School Booklist. *Your Reading: A Booklist for Junior High and Middle School Students.* 8th ed. National Council of Teachers of English, 1991.

Patros, P. and T. Shamoo. *Depression and Suicide in Children and Adolescents.* Allyn and Bacon, 1989.

Stupple, D. M. "Rx for the Suicide Epidemic," *English Journal,* January, 1987, p. 64 ff.

Joan Kaywell, University of South Florida, Tampa

ALL THE FACTS— AND THE FICTION

Here's a way to combine new fiction for junior high students with topics for library investigation. Our obliging librarian welcomed the opportunity to get new fiction into the hands of readers, and together we made a list of novels dealing with problems faced by adolescents of the eighties: divorce, alcohol, drugs, handicaps, child abuse, adoption, abortion, to name a few. (*Your Reading* and *Books for You,* both NCTE publications, are useful resources in compiling a list of adolescent fiction dealing with social problems.) Among the books we used were Judy Blume's *It's Not the End of the World,* dealing with divorce; Paula Danziger's *The Cat Ate My Gymsuit,* being fat and having school problems; James Forman's *A Fine, Soft Day,* the Protestant-Catholic conflict in Belfast; Michelle Magorian's *Good Night, Mr. Tom,* child abuse; Kin Platt's *The Boy Who Could Make Himself Disappear,* speech and communication disabilities. Each ninth-grader chose a novel, read it (usually eagerly!), and then prepared to investigate the social or personal problem dealt with in the novel.

Each student was to jot down at least two direct quotations from the novel he or she had read, a quote that might prove useful in introducing or concluding a research paper on the problem dealt with in the novel—an observation by the author or perhaps a bit of trenchant dialogue. Brief notes were also to be made about main characters, setting, and the fictionalized treatment of the problem, especially how honestly the author dealt with the problem. One question to be considered was whether or not the problem was solved too simply—that is, the main character merely concludes, "Okay, tomorrow I'll go to Ala-Teen and get rid of my drinking problem." Or did the author deal truthfully with the struggle that was to come or the fact that some problems would remain unsolved?

Students then spent three or four days in the library, investigating the problems dealt with in the novels they had read. Magazine articles located through the *Readers' Guide to Periodical Literature, Newsbank* selections from newspapers, and nonfiction books provided the information base for their research papers.

I found this strategy particularly useful in generating enthusiasm about the topics to be researched. Students enjoyed reading the new fiction and were interested in expanding and verifying their insights through research. The quotations from the novels provided ready-made introductions or effective conclusions for their papers. The results were by far the best research papers ever turned in to me!

Mary M. Burman, Laramie Junior High School, Laramie, Wyoming

NOT JUST ANOTHER BOOK TALK

This book talk is a special part of a unit on values in society. Before discussing the values that society encourages in teenagers (honesty, loyalty, industry, thrift, etc.), students explore children's literature to discover what values are encouraged in young children. I ask students to follow these steps:

1. Choose and read a children's book—preferably one written for an audience of four- to six-year olds. You will be reading this book aloud to the class, so length should also be a consideration.
2. Write a paragraph to introduce the book to the class. Remember to mention the book's title and author.
3. Find three values (qualities that are held important, such as honesty, loyalty, hard work, etc.) that are strongly stressed throughout the book.
4. Write a short paragraph in which you explain the three values encouraged in the book. You will need to explain and give examples of *how* each value is reinforced in the story (pictures, description of characters, dialogue, etc.).
5. Your presentation should last between five and eight minutes. As you read, you may share the pictures with the class if you wish.

This activity encourages students to speak confidently in front of their peers, and the simplicity of the texts means that even hesitant readers can enjoy the assignment.

Beth Chaney, Walnut Springs Middle School, Westerville, Ohio

HOMOPHOBIA: THEME OF THE NOVEL *JACK*

Faggot!" reverberates down the corridor. Homosexual labels are common terms of disparagement at the school where I teach. Speakers may not intend to question the sexual orientation of classmates—they use such terms loosely, as general insults—but even so, I'm often aware of some student who shrinks in discomfort. I'm bothered by my students' callous attitudes concerning homosexuality.

While listening to National Public Radio, I heard a review of a book, written for adolescents, about a teenager whose father left the family after he realized he was gay. The reviewer said the book was well-written, sensitive, and enlightening. I grabbed a pen in time to write down the title and author: *Jack*, by A. M. Homes.

I read *Jack* and decided it was easy and engaging enough for the "at-risk" students I teach. I agreed with the reviewer that the book has literary merit; it is worth teaching apart from the fact that it addresses an issue that concerns me. To secure support from my school's administrators, should anyone object to *Jack*, I sent a statement to them, explaining that I wanted to teach a book that does not advocate homosexuality but that does dramatize the suffering that may result from intolerance.

At home I imagined that I might receive irate, accusing telephone calls, so I searched for a pamphlet I recall stashing years ago called *A Student's Right to Read*, published by NCTE. I never did find my pamphlet, but I didn't need it. The only objection my students raised about *Jack* is that it is too young for them. The hero of the book is only fifteen; most of my students are about seventeen; so those who want a protagonist their own age are right. I recommend using this book with younger students.

My students answered the following questions about *Jack*, working in either small, cooperative groups or singly, as they preferred. Originally the only question under "A" was number five, but I found that students from homes where violent behavior is routine had difficulty evaluating the fathers' behaviors. I added questions one through four; working through them helped those students see that the gay father is more caring than the heterosexual father.

CHARACTERIZATION, PLOT, THEME, POINT OF VIEW, AND SETTING

After reading all of the novel, *Jack*, by A. M. Homes,

A. Contrast Jack's father, Paul, with Max's father, Mr. Burka. Support your generalizations by listing specific acts each did.

1. What does Mr. Burka do to and for Mrs. Burka?
2. What does Paul do to and for Jack's mom?
3. List each fatherly act by Mr. Burka.
4. List each fatherly act by Paul.

From here on, please answer in complete sentences.

5. Compare Paul and Mr. Burka as people and as fathers. Which is better? Why?

(This answer, written by a two-student team, was typical: *"Paul is a better person and has much to contribute to society rather than Mr. Burka. Paul is compassionate, affectionate, open and honest when dealing with his feelings. Mr. Burka treats his family as if they were all in the military. He also suppresses his feelings until they explode with physical violence. Paul is continually spending quality time with Jack. Mr. Burka spends quantity time but not quality time with his sons."*)

B. What is the main idea, the theme, expressed in this book? In other words, what is the author's message?

(This question was the one I most wanted insightful answers to, and I was pleased. For example: *"I think the intention of this book was to help people understand the differences in others. I was left with a better idea of what homosexuality is and that people don't necessarily choose to be gay. Also that if people are gay they shouldn't try to cover it up. A person's sexual preference doesn't change who they really are."*

Another group wrote: *"Don't judge a book by its cover but, by what is in the inside. The theme is that people who are not norm to society are often better people than the norm of our society. The idea is not to judge people by what they are but by the actions in which they chose to deal with other people."*)

C. *Jack* is written in first person. The author used the pronoun "I" rather than the pronoun "he," and the story is told from the point of view of the main character. What are some advantages in writing this novel in first person?
D. The author set her novel in contemporary, middle-class suburban America. Speculate about why she chose this setting instead of some other.

Jack succeeds in causing students to look at their own assumptions and attitudes. In this way, and in its use of the vernacular, it possesses some of the strengths of *Huckleberry Finn.* I would like to teach *Jack* along with *To Kill a Mockingbird* and *Catcher in the Rye* and ask my students to compare these books. A colleague suggested that I could include *Coming of Age in Mississippi* by Anne Moody.

Complementary writing assignments could be about people the students have known who were "picked on" at school or elsewhere. My writing students always have a repertoire of experiences on this topic.

I was relieved and surprised that only one student expressed offense from *Jack*; he confided his feelings to me after class, saying, "It sucks." A few others said it was a good book; but, as I mentioned earlier, a few thought it should be read by younger students. At term's end I was delighted when, to the course evaluation question "Of the areas covered in this course, which aspects will be of greatest use to you?" an anonymous student wrote, "The novel *Jack* because it showed me another point of view towards gay people than just calling them fags."

Nan Phifer, Lane Community College Adult High School, Eugene, Oregon

THE CALL OF ADVENTURE
Jack London's "To Build a Fire"

It was no longer a mere matter of freezing his fingers and toes, or of losing his hands and feet, but . . . it was a matter of life and death with the chances against him.

—Jack London, "To Build a Fire," 1902

One subject that has nearly universal appeal for teenagers is adventure. In fact, for many young people, just the mention of the word conjures images of excitement and danger, strange and exotic settings in far-off lands, and heroes who take risks and perform brave deeds. Yet while our teenage students may be quick to see the glamorous possibilities of adventure stories popularized by television and films, they are not so quick to consider that besides revealing the best in people, these stories also reveal the worst. Adventure stories show human strengths *and* weaknesses.

Fortunately, students' interest in the subject draws them to some of the excellent literature that explores the possible negative consequences of people failing to listen to sound advice and common sense and being tested to the limits of their abilities under extreme circumstances. Jack London's regularly anthologized short story "To Build a Fire" (from his collection of short stories

To Build a Fire and Other Stories by Jack London [Bantam Classic, 1986]) is a story of wilderness survival that addresses the naive notions of young people who would ignore the lessons inherent in wisdom and experience and blindly rely on only their own abilities. The main character is a vain young man who ignores the sound advice given to him by an old-timer and believes that he knows the frozen wilderness. But he is actually still a tenderfoot who has not yet learned to respect the power of nature.

Most secondary teachers are familiar with this story about a young man's futile attempt to travel across ten miles of Yukon wilderness in temperatures dropping to seventy-five degrees below zero. The unnamed protagonist, whose only companion is his wolf-dog, realizes too late the wisdom in the old-timer's warnings never to travel alone during the harsh winter. In his ignorance, the tenderfoot had laughed at the old-timer's advice. But caught in the bitter cold, the young man begins to understand the value of the old man's warning. "To Build a Fire" suggests to students the dangers in ignoring advice based on wisdom and experience and in placing too much faith in one's self and one's ability to cope in very difficult situations.

But there are other important reasons for studying this story. The man's egotism conflicts with his common sense. He does not understand the frailty of humans and is too proud to admit his own. He does not comprehend the danger posed by an alien, hostile environment in which he can only survive by the full exercise of his wit, instincts, skill, and cunning. The story challenges students to consider their place in the scheme of things and to respect the power of nature; it demands that students examine their own views and gain insight into the views of others. Finally, students begin to understand the importance of good judgment, experience, and common sense when faced with extreme conditions in the wilderness.

This story might also serve as a starting point for students who plan to read a series of short stories and longer works in which the characters must battle hostile forces in order to survive. For example, in addition to reading "To Build a Fire," students might read Carl Stephenson's "Leininger versus the Ants," Daphne du Maurier's "The Birds," Stephen Vincent Benét's "By the Waters of Babylon," Barbara Kimenye's "The Winner," John McPhee's "A Postponed Death," J. Nutuko Nzioki's "Not Meant for Young Ears," and a longer work such as Daniel Defoe's *Robinson Crusoe*, Claude Brown's *Manchild in the Promised Land*, Willa Cather's *O Pioneers!*, or Robert Louis Stevenson's *Treasure Island*.

In addition, while adventure stories are a mainstay of young adult literature, many students have not seriously studied this literature, despite finding it exciting and enjoyable. Therefore, another important reason to have students read "To Build a Fire" is to provide them with an opportunity to study a key element of this kind of fiction, as well as of literature in general: irony.

EXPLORING STUDENT VIEWS

I begin with an activity that uses students' ideas and opinions about survival in the wilderness. Before students read the story, I ask them to fill out a handout sheet entitled "Wilderness Survival Opinionnaire." (See page 50.) Although the items on the opinionnaire are often stated in absolute terms, students can be encouraged to respond holistically, based on whether they are fundamentally inclined to agree or disagree with each statement.

After students have responded to all the statements on the opinionnaire, I list the results on the board. Then, beginning with the statements for which there is the most disagreement, we discuss their responses to each statement. I encourage students to explain the reasoning behind their responses and to debate differing opinions. Since the statements on the opinionnaire require students to take a stand, a lively discussion invariably ensues.

One purpose of the opinionnaire and follow-up discussion is to create interest in the characters and issues developed in the story the students are about to read. Statements 10, 11, and 12, for example, relate to one aspect of the problem that the tenderfoot faces in the story. At the beginning of the tale, the young man underestimates the extreme conditions he faces: he is aware that his face and fingers are slightly numb from the cold, but he fails to realize the seriousness of his circumstances. Soon, when he stops to eat lunch, he begins to wish that he had foreseen the danger of frostbite and brought a facial strap for protection. He convinces himself that frostbitten cheeks are never serious, merely painful, as a way to soothe himself psychologically and to force himself not to worry about the cold. The tenderfoot then builds a fire to warm himself, and, as the fire restores his confidence, he laughs at the warning of the old-timer from Sulphur Creek, the warning about traveling alone in extreme conditions. It is not until the very end of the story, until just before the young man dies, that he admits to himself that the old man at Sulphur Creek had been right.

Student responses to the statements on the opinionnaire usually indicate that, like the tenderfoot in the story, many of them underestimate the power of nature. Also, just like the young man in the story, many teenagers disdain taking advice from others about how to survive in the wilderness.

During class discussion about these statements, students often point to popular media heroes such as Indiana Jones who seem to be quite self-reliant. These young heroes seem able to survive any difficult situation without advice from anyone. London indicates that when youthful pride and self-confidence ignore the sound advice of wisdom and experience, the result could be self-destruction. It is through class discussion of these and other statements from the opinionnaire that students begin to question some of their initial responses and are motivated to find out how the character will deal with these issues in the story.

Another purpose of the opinionnaire is to provide a framework or context that will help students overcome some of their initial difficulty with the long narrative passages in "To Build a Fire." London's brand of storytelling in this particular tale depends upon the cold, objective presentation of detail that respects the force and power of nature and reduces the individual.to a position of relative insignificance. As a result, the story begins with and contains long narrative passages that many students have difficulty getting through. Yet through discussion of the items on the opinionnaire, students become better prepared for what they find in the story.

The framework that the opinionnaire provides also helps students to understand what London wants readers to learn about the potential danger of failing to recognize our own frailties and failing to respect the awesome power of nature. Many students readily dismiss statement 3, that humans cannot win against nature. They point to the many ways that humans have tamed nature, particularly with technology. During discussion about this and other related statements on the opinionnaire, though, students are often surprised to discover that some of their classmates do not share their optimism regarding humans' ability to control nature. Some students point to blizzards, floods, earthquakes, and other natural disasters as examples of people's inability to control nature. Additionally, in discussing statements 1, 6, and 14, students are encouraged to consider a wide range of ideas related to survival in the wilderness. As we discuss the various student-generated ideas, they begin to think about nature in new ways and to consider what it really takes to survive in the wilderness. These and other questions help students construct a framework or cognitive map that will better enable them to understand the story they are about to read.

Once we have discussed most or all of the statements on the opinionnaire, I collect them for later use. I then ask students to read the story. I usually request that they read part of the story aloud. I read the first couple of pages to them and then I call on students, preferably volunteers, to read a few paragraphs aloud while the rest of the class silently follows along. We continue in this fashion up to the point just *before* the snow falls from the spruce tree and blots out the tenderfoot's last fire.

EXAMINING THE MAIN CHARACTER AND PREDICTING THE OUTCOME

At this point, I ask students to complete the opinionnaire for a second time, this time from the point of view of the main character in the story. In other words, I ask them to mark the statements the way they think the young man would. Then I lead a class discussion of their responses. This discussion is nearly as lively as the one in which we discuss their own viewpoints.

In discussing how the tenderfoot would respond to the statements on the opinionnaire, most students see him as being brave with a touch of good luck. They admire him because he takes risks, and they believe, as statement 7 says, that his bravery will enable him to overcome whatever obstacles he encounters. They point to the fact that despite the old-timer's warnings, the tenderfoot is managing just fine without a partner and in very cold conditions. These students are surprised to discover that a few students in the class are actually convinced that the tenderfoot is a fool. They point to the fact that the dog appears frightened and nervous about moving away from the fire, and the dog's behavior should be enough to show the man that he has underestimated the danger of the tremendously low temperatures. This, they argue, shows that he is so full of himself that he is ignoring common sense. I also use this discussion as an opportunity to make sure students have a basic understanding of the plot and setting of the story.

I conclude this discussion by asking students to predict how they think the story will end. Perhaps influenced by popular adventure films, the majority of students believe that the tenderfoot will be faced with some final test of his skill and bravery, such as being attacked by a bear, but that he will survive and make it to the camp where his friends are waiting for him. A smaller group of students believe that the man has acted foolishly and will more than likely not survive his journey. They argue that even after all that has happened to him, the man does not really appreciate the danger of his situation.

With their interest ignited, I ask students to finish the rest of the story on their own. I suggest to them that they keep in mind the ideas we have discussed.

THE AUTHOR'S MESSAGE AND THE STUDENTS' LIVES

Once students have finished reading the story, they are prepared to deal with irony and with what the author is telling us about survival in the wilderness and about human nature. We divide into small groups, and I ask students to determine from evidence in the story how London would probably respond to the statements on the opinionnaire. In addition, I ask students to determine what actually killed the tenderfoot. Was it just blind luck? Is he somehow responsible for what happened to him? Or is it something else? In other words, what is London saying about survival in the wilderness and about human nature?

After resolving their responses to these questions, the students reassemble to discuss and debate their findings. As the groups report their answers, students begin to formulate important conclusions. They realize, for example, that the old-timer was right about traveling without a partner. If the protagonist in the story had had a partner with him when the snow blotted out his fire, his partner would have been able to restart the fire, which the young man was unable to do because his hands were frozen. Student also realize that luck has nothing to do with the tenderfoot's death, and that survival in the wilderness depends not upon youth and self-confidence but upon wisdom and experience. Additionally, students recognize London's message that humans must respect the power of nature and understand our own human frailties.

Discussing the statements on the opinionnaire in terms of what London would probably say about them is an important element in helping students interpret the irony and formulate important conclusions about the story. For example, it is through this discussion that many students come to see that, while the tenderfoot might agree that "It is better to make your own mistakes than to listen to advice from others" (statement 10), London would probably not agree with this statement, particularly with regard to survival in the wilderness. In fact, London is suggesting exactly the opposite.

Once the class has discussed most or all of the statements in terms of how the author would probably have responded to them, I ask students to complete the opinionnaire once again. When they have filled it out, I pass out the opinionnaire students completed before they read the story and ask them to compare their answers. Often opinions have changed. For example, some students who had previously regarded a brave person as someone who takes risks (statements 2 and 5) and is able to overcome all obstacles (statement 7) now regarded risk taking and attempting to overcome obstacles in the wilderness in severe weather conditions as acts of foolishness. In contrast to their previous views, many of these students now felt that the wise course of action would be to seek advice from those who have experience. Students begin to see the impact that the story has had on them.

FOLLOW-UP ACTIVITIES

In discussing which statements on the opinionnaire London would probably agree or disagree with and why, we find considerable disagreement about some statements. This disagreement provides a natural follow-up writing exercise. I ask students to write a composition explaining why they think London would agree or disagree with one of the statements with which the class is having a problem. I encourage them to write it in the form of a letter to one of the students in the class who disagrees with their viewpoint.

Another possible follow-up activity is to have students read, on their own, another story in which a character must battle hostile forces in order to survive, a story that uses irony to convey its meaning. Then I ask the students to write an interpretation of the story. I use either Richard Connell's regularly anthologized "The Most Dangerous Game" (1924) or Arthur Gordon's "The Sea Devil" (1953).

I also give students an opportunity to rewrite the ending of the story. I ask them to imagine that the tenderfoot manages to restart the fire that the falling snow put out. I encourage them to answer the following questions in their new ending: What will the tenderfoot do once he is dried off and warmed by the fire? What will his attitude be toward the old-timer? Why? What will his attitude be toward the wolf-dog? Why? Will the tenderfoot survive? If so, how? If not, why not?

Discussing how student attitudes have changed as a result of reading the story also provides a natural follow-up writing environment, particularly for students who might be caught up in the popular images of adventure heroes. I ask them to write a composition in which they explain how and why their opinion has changed about two of the statements on the opinionnaire after reading the story. I ask them to explain what their opinion was before reading the story and why, what their opinion was after reading it, and I ask them to provide supporting evidence from the story to explain any change in attitude. These follow-up activities reinforce skills students have developed in reading and analyzing "To Build a Fire." They also serve as a means to determine their mastery of those skills.

Larry R. Johannessen, St. Xavier University, Chicago, Illinois

Wilderness Survival Opinionnaire

Directions: Read each of the following statements. Write "A" if you agree with the statement or "D" if you disagree with it.

Agree or Disagree

_____ 1. Only the fittest survive in the wilderness.

_____ 2. It is better to take risks in life than to be too cautious.

_____ 3. Humans cannot win against nature.

_____ 4. Most people deserve their fate.

_____ 5. True heroes put themselves in dangerous situations and then get out of them.

_____ 6. People should listen to their instincts, especially in the wilderness.

_____ 7. A brave person can overcome all obstacles.

_____ 8. A little knowledge is a dangerous thing.

_____ 9. Animals are smarter than people.

_____ 10. It is better to make your own mistakes than to listen to advice from others.

_____ 11. Frostbitten fingers are not life-threatening in the wilderness.

_____ 12. People who ignore other people's advice are self-reliant and smart.

_____ 13. It is better not to think about our problems.

_____ 14. There is no such thing as luck when it comes to survival in the wilderness. People have to make their own luck if they expect to survive.

_____ 15. Physical strength is the most important quality needed for a person to survive in the wilderness.

_____ 16. Survival in subzero temperatures depends on thinking through each problem carefully.

_____ 17. Intelligence is the key to survival in harsh conditions.

_____ 18. Careful planning is the most important thing when it comes to survival in subzero temperatures.

_____ 19. Always expect the worst to happen in the wilderness.

_____ 20. Luck is just as important as anything else when it comes to survival in extreme conditions.

THE AIM GAME

The AIM Game is a prereading sequence in three parts, geared towards involving students in activities that will make their reading a short story more interesting—and more perceptive.

The teacher pre-selects an appropriate theme and one or more stories that deal with the theme. In the example below, the theme is the relationship between human beings and modern technology. Possible short stories include Donald Barthelme's "Report," Ray Bradbury's "The Rocket Man," Frank Brown's "Singing Dinah's Song," Robert F. Young's "Thirty Days Had September," and Kurt Vonnegut's "Epicac." (There are dozens of other stories, of course, on the humanity/technology theme.)

As the game progresses, students create their own vocabulary list of words related to the theme, explore relation words on the vocabulary list, and exchange opinions with regard to the theme. The AIM Game—which usually takes three to four class periods—has three steps:

1. *Associating Ideas.* A brainstorming activity in which students in small groups play two word-association games using words related to the theme.
2. *Ideas that Match.* A relationship-making exercise in which students, using the two word lists generated in Step 1, make up five pairs of words by matching words from their first word-association list with words from their second word-association list.
3. *My Opinion, Your Opinion.* A discussion game in which students explain why they agree or disagree with five "Opinion Statements" related to the theme.

Associating Ideas

Divide your class into groups of four or five students. Ask each group to appoint a recorder who will write down the words called out by other group members. Then give the groups ninety seconds to brainstorm as many words as possible associated with the word "computer." When time is up, the recorder for each group counts and reads aloud the words generated by the group. Have students repeat the process above, using a different sheet of paper to list words that they associate with the word "freedom."

Ideas that Match

Have the students in each group match up five words from their "computer" list with five words from their "freedom" list. Unlike the brainstorming game, this step is untimed, and the students should be able to explain in their own words *how* each of the five word-pairs is justified. For example, the students in a group might match the word *document* from their "computer" list with the word *Constitution* from their "freedom" list. They should be able to support the matchup if called upon to do so, with a statement like "The U.S. Constitution is a kind of document"—a categorization relationship according to specific example/general type.

A member of each group should write the five word pairs on the chalkboard so other groups can read them and ask for an explanation of the relationships that aren't obvious. The nature of the matchup can be any kind of relationship—synonymity, anonymity, categorization, cause-effect, analogy, etc.—that can be explained informally by the students in a group.

My Opinion, Your Opinion

Write the following Opinion Statements on the chalkboard, or give students copies of the statements. Ask them to read silently and decide, on an individual basis, whether they *agree* or *disagree* with each statement.

Circle the "A" if you agree with the statement. Circle the "D" if you disagree.

A D   1. The world of the future will be a better place for humanity.
A D   2. With computers and machines playing such a big part in our lives, we have a tendency to lose contact with nature.
A D   3. Humanity can dream great dreams, but they aren't likely to come true.
A D   4. Someday computers and machines will free us from hard labor.
A D   5. Computers and machines could become so important in our lives that they would actually rule us.

Discuss each statement with the class, asking initially how many agreed and how many disagreed. Don't try to arrive at a "right" answer, but encourage the students to explain why they felt as they did, exchanging ideas freely on each of the statements. Often, students will change their opinions during the course of the discussion as the statements are examined closely and the students explore their feelings more fully.

The students are now ready to read Barthelme's "Report," or a similar story on the theme of humans and technology. Note that in Step 1, the students created their own vocabulary list of words associated with themes in the unit. (Teachers report that words on the students' lists often appear in the short story, in fact.) In Step 2, the students' thinking skills were challenged as they put together (often humorously or ingeniously) pairs of words associated with the theme. In Step 3, they clarified their own ideas on crucial issues that the author raises in the story. The students themselves, in a sense, are "authors" of words and ideas on how human beings relate to technology. They are prepared to experience Barthelme's exploration of the theme.

Charles Suhor, Urbana, Illinois

3 | EMPHASIS: FROM RESPONSE TO CRITICISM

ENGAGING STUDENTS IN WRITING ABOUT CHARACTER

The character Squeaky, in Toni Cade Bambara's short story "Raymond's Run," never fails to intrigue my eighth-grade language arts students. They understand the change that takes place in a few moments at the end of the story, when, as she waits to hear whether she or her rival has won the annual May Day race, Squeaky matures into someone able to see from other people's perspectives and to accept not always being "first." Perhaps it's because my students see a part of themselves or their friends in Squeaky, or perhaps it's because of her strength and determination. Whatever it is, Squeaky is a perfect character to use when I want to engage my students in close interaction with the text to produce lively and insightful written assignments. I have also used this assignment with other dynamic literary characters with equally successful results, and friends who teach in grade school have used a modified version with great results. All my students have experienced success with these activities and seem to enjoy both the group and individual work required of them.

I begin by having students predict what the story may be about by reading just the title. This will be the first entry in their journals. As we read the story, the students continue to write in their journals whenever they feel it is necessary. We briefly discuss the predictions, and curiosity seems high as we begin reading the story aloud, trading off between student volunteer readers and me. We continue by moving into small, randomly selected groups, with each member of the group reading aloud to the others. Periodically, group members choose to stop and discuss the readings and make journal entries. This helps students reflect on and make sense of what has been read. It usually takes two days to read the story this way.

The third day begins with a quickwrite about Squeaky. Students then trade writings, and each reads one other quickwrite, followed by a brainstorming session, in which I list all the details the students tell me about Squeaky.

The rest of the lesson is taken up with a group activity. Students are grouped into fours. Each group uses a large sheet of butcher paper and marker pens to answer a different question about Squeaky that I have written on a note card for them.

Here are sample questions that encourage personal response as well as information:

Group Questions
    How does Squeaky feel?
    How does Squeaky treat people she likes?
    What does Squeaky say?
    How do other characters react to what Squeaky says?
    How did you react to what she says?
    What does Squeaky learn?

I form other questions based on the sentence starters on the "Character Analysis" handout (see below).

I encourage the groups to use the text to help develop their answers, which are then written on the butcher paper. After three or four minutes, all groups are asked to rotate clockwise to the next table, where they will read the next question, answer it, and write the answer on the butcher paper below the previous group's answer. This technique lets students see that there are several possible answers to each question. The group rotation continues until there are four or five different answers to the same question on each piece of butcher paper. This part of the activity can get a little noisy, but the students have fun moving around and reading the answers already on the paper.

When all the groups have had a chance to answer all the questions, the designated reporter for each group will read aloud the answers on their own piece of paper, and then the group will tape the paper to the wall. After all groups have shared their answers, I allow a few minutes of free discussion and interaction; then, as a closure activity, I ask students to write in their journals something special they liked about Squeaky.

We begin the fourth day by discussing the previous day's work and reviewing journals for several minutes. Students may do this silently or with a partner. Alternatively they may ask questions or make comments on the story at this time. Next, I distribute a "Character Analysis" handout containing the following guidelines.

Character Analysis

In "Raymond's Run," Squeaky is shown to be a complex character. As the story progresses, she grows and changes while revealing several sides to her personality. Finally, Squeaky reaches a new awareness and makes a clear choice about the kind of person she wants to be. The many details revealed in the story make Squeaky come alive and seem like a real person.

Use these details, and what you learned in your groups, to complete the following sentences. Remember to look in the book for even more ideas, and check carefully if you plan to use some direct quotations.

Squeaky thinks . . .
Squeaky sees life . . .
Squeaky treats people she likes . . .
Squeaky treats people she dislikes . . .
Squeaky feels . . .
Squeaky says . . .
Squeaky acts like . . .
Squeaky likes . . .
Squeaky dislikes . . .
Squeaky gives . . .
Squeaky values . . .
Squeaky learns . . .
Squeaky's future will be . . .

Now that you have completed the sentences, draw your idea of Squeaky on plain white paper and rewrite the sentences around the picture. Finally, color the picture before handing your work in.

The students quickly realize that the questions used in the group activity provide the information needed for this part of the activity. Knowing that they have already done much of the work makes even reluctant writers more relaxed, and consequently, more willing to produce a quality piece of work. I always add a few more statements than questions to challenge those that need or want to be challenged. Completing these is optional. Many students will do more than required and delve into the text to find even more to write about Squeaky. This part of the assignment usually takes two days to complete.

The results I obtain with this activity are truly exhilarating, as I see higher-level thinking skills being used to carefully analyze the character and produce some very detailed pieces of work. I must mention that the artistic interpretations are varied and wonderful, too. One student chose to draw a picture of Raymond instead of Squeaky. Could it be that asking students to draw something, without being judgmental, encourages some to write more carefully and thoughtfully after creating such beautiful and varied interpretations of the characters? I always display *all* student work on this assignment, because it is so varied, and so good.

Then I assign a one-day in-class writing assignment, because I feel students know Squeaky very well at this point. A sample approach, using a "Writing Situation" handout, is shown below. Students may also suggest and pursue alternate ideas for writing assignments, with teacher approval.

I allow students to use the text, their dialectical journals, their quickwrites, and the work on the walls to inspire them. Again, quality work results, because the students are fully engaged in Squeaky and her life.

Writing Situation

In "Raymond's Run," by Toni Cade Bambara, Squeaky learns a number of valuable lessons in life while running and winning the May Day race once again.

Think about what happened to Squeaky that day. Imagine that you are Squeaky and you want to write about your experience. Do one of the following:

1. Write a letter to Gretchen explaining how your feelings toward her have changed, and why. Explain how you want your relationship to proceed from this point on, and why you feel that way.
2. Write a letter to Raymond explaining how your relationship with him has changed, and why. Explain your plans for the future for both of you.
3. Develop your own idea for writing and check it with me.

Begin with a freewrite or make a list of details from the story that support your ideas. Next, organize your ideas around a good thesis statement. It would be a good idea to use a bubble cluster to help you organize at this point.

Write the first draft, making sure you use paragraphs to organize your ideas. Revise carefully and make thoughtful changes to clarify and improve your essay. Finally, proofread your work for spelling, grammar, and punctuation before writing your best final draft.

To generate thoughtful and meaningful writing assignments, students must be fully engaged with the text. The realistically strong yet very sensitive

Squeaky is the perfect vehicle for rewarding and worthwhile literary engagement.

Shirley Chambers, Auburndale Intermediate School, Corona, California

RESPONDING TO HEROES AND HEROINES

Because many adolescents want to find someone they can admire, and like to imagine being heroes or heroines themselves, I use reading and supplementary activities to help students to develop a clear understanding of what a hero or heroine is. As Joseph Campbell has said, the heroic figure has a thousand faces. Heroes and heroines are found not only in myths and fantasy, but also in young adult literature, science fiction, historical and contemporary fiction, and biographies. Whatever the genre, students will attach more meaning to the concept of hero and heroine if they are able to form personal responses to what they are reading. The following array of activities allows students to choose how they want to respond to ideas from their reading--whether by writing a dialogue, role-playing a scene, evaluating a film, talking with peers, keeping a response journal, or other ways.

1. Interview a parent, relative, or friend to find out who his or her heroes are and why.
2. Give your own personal definitions of *hero* and *heroine* and of words associated with heroes, such as *courage, victory, self-sacrifice, struggle,* and *integrity.* If you like, you may illustrate with examples from your own experience.
3. Write a metaphor in response to the question, "What is a hero or heroine?" (For example, "a hero is an oak tree" or "a hero is a Saturn rocket.") Then explain why. Use details that continue the metaphor

(for example, "an oak has acorns that will grow to be oaks, and a hero has followers who will try to take on his or her characteristics.")

4. While reading a novel about a hero or heroine, write journal entries in response to these questions:

    What was the hero's greatest difficulty? How did the way he or she handled it show heroism?

    What must an individual do or not do to be considered a hero?

    If a hero were faced with a particular problem (state it), how would he or she handle it?

    Is there such a thing as a quiet hero who goes unrecognized by others? Explain.

5. Join a literature study group of students who are reading the same book you are. Keep a literature response log while you read. As a group, plan a culminating experience for the class that relates in some way to the book or to what you have learned from the book.

6. Write a journal or diary of several entries from the perspective of the hero or heroine of your book or of someone who knew him or her.

7. Find and read an article in a recent magazine or newspaper about a person whom you would call a hero or heroine. Write a paragraph explaining your reasons for choosing this person.

8. Select an incident from the book you're reading (either fiction or nonfiction would be appropriate) in which someone behaves heroically. Write a newspaper account of this incident.

9. Write a letter to the hero or heroine explaining what you think about him or her and why.

10. After reading a story or nonfiction account, write a letter from the point of view of the hero or heroine to an appropriate audience or to the class.

11. Write a letter from one character to another explaining the motive behind a particular action.

12. Write a letter either about or to a hero or heroine, from the vantage point of twenty or more years in the future.

13. Select a "Hero or Heroine of the Day." Write an explanation of your reasons for granting the award to a particular person. If you like, photograph your hero or heroine in an appropriate outfit or costume.

14. Role-play a scene where a person acts heroically. The idea for the scene could be from your imaginations, from life, or from literature. You may enlist the help of a partner or partners if needed.

15. Plan a "hero reception" with yourself playing the role of a hero/heroine you have been reading about.

16. Select a scene from something we have read about a hero or heroine

and convert the scene to a television, radio, or a dramatic script. Or use mime, finger puppets, or a dance to present the scene.

17. Write about ways in which the hero or heroine's life parallels your own life.

18. Write a poem about a particular hero or a heroine.

19. Write a story continuation after reading only the first part of a story. Then read the author's ending and compare and contrast your version with the author's.

20. Write the first chapter of a novel or a nonfiction account about a hero or heroine, perhaps with illustrations.

21. Evaluate a videotape of a recent film to decide whether or not the main character is a hero or heroine. (As a model, use Joseph Campbell's analysis of *Star Wars* in "The Hero's Adventure," Part I from the series entitled, *Joseph Campbell and the Power of Myth* [Mystic Fire Video].)

22. Write a dialogue that you would like to have with the hero or heroine. If you like, find a partner and practice the dialogue, taking both parts in turn.

23. Write observations of our culture from the point of view of a hero from the past or a hero from a different culture.

24. Write a biographical sketch of one of your heroes, either from the past or the present.

25. Design a crest for the hero or heroine of the book you are reading with at least three symbolic representations of his or her heroic qualities. Write an explanation of the symbolism in your crest and how it relates to the hero or heroine.

26. Draw the hero or heroine in the story you are reading.

27. Write a letter to a movie director suggesting which scenes from a novel about a hero or heroine would make a good screen play and why.

28. With a partner, write a script of your critical opinions of a novel about a hero or heroine or of the film based on the novel. Follow the format of television reviews of current movies in which two reviewers give their opinions. Then videotape your presentation.

29. Write and videotape a biographical sketch of a famous hero or heroine.

30. Rewrite the story, in summary form, from the viewpoint of another character. In conclusion, write a paragraph about how this change in viewpoint affects the theme.

These possibilities have stimulated both thoughtful and creative responses from my students.

Eleanor Gaunder, University of North Alabama, Florence

LITERARY DINNER PARTIES

For the past few years, my students and I have been inviting authors and characters to our classroom for dinner parties and lively conversations in a writing project we call "Literary Dinner Parties." With this approach, I motivate eighth graders into completing written book projects by letting them talk and eat at the same time, two of their favorite pastimes.

I first ask my students to read novels which interest them and to become familiar with the characters and authors they will be portraying. As they read, they write commentary in their literary journals, both on their own and with my instruction. Since they read their novels outside of class, I use class time to introduce writing dialogue and conversation. To discover how the authors' use of dialogue enlivens characters and enhances stories, we read and study the following stories (all found in *Adventures for Readers* [the Heritage Edition, Book 2]):

"Charles," by Shirley Jackson
"A Cap for Steve," by Morley Callaghan
"Thank You, M'am," by Langston Hughes
"Then He Goes Free," by Jessamyn West
"The Street," by Richard Wright

Once students have become familiar with the rudiments of writing conversation, I ask them to write various dialogues in their journals: a telephone conversation with a friend, a family dinner conversation, a conversation with a pet or an inanimate object, a conversation with an adult, any dialogue which reveals some aspect of the speaker's character rather than being random or overly literal. We share our conversations in response group activities, seeking support and receiving suggestions.

As their out-of-class reading continues and their dialogue expertise grows, I ask my students to focus upon writing dialogues with the characters and authors of their review format. My students are required to write conversations between themselves and their characters or their authors while they are dining together and turn those in as their reviews. To help my students feel part of the conversation and to relieve their anxiety, I tell them to write their narratives in first-person, as if they were writing in their journals or telling someone a story. This eases their tension and lets them develop their personal perceptions of the characters' and authors' attitudes, lifestyles, actions, and philosophies. By becoming part of the social activity, eighth graders pay closer attention to detail, to describing the setting, to the participants, and to the action in their own voices.

Because a good host or hostess knows that dinner parties require much preparation, I require such preparation from my students. After I have taught informal letter writing, I have my students write invitations to their guests stating the time, place, and reason for the dinner. These dinners may take place anywhere from Paris to a country picnic, and the invitations can reflect those settings. Addressing envelopes to certain individuals has proved taxing for some students, but many have used their imaginations and pulled ideas from their novels.

In addition to the written activities for their dinner party, I ask the students to create menus for the specific meals they will serve. Involving the home economics and art teachers in this part of the project is helpful, for I want the students to develop well-balanced meals and construct artistic menus as souvenirs for themselves and their guests. My students must consider the specific needs or tastes of their guests as they complete this exercise, so their menus show me how well they have read their books. I'm always amazed at what character prefers peanut butter to lobster tail and that tartar steak has become steak à la King or Coquilles St. Jacques has been renamed Coquilles St. Orwell.

When the final day arrives and all projects are due, I conduct a small dinner party in my classroom. Madeleine L'Engle arrives in a red Jaguar, Stephen King meets Edgar Allan Poe, James Herriot pets the family dog, Anne Frank discusses her writing style, and Hester Prynne corrects Pearl's table manners. Students bring samples from their menus to share with the class. While we feast, we read journals, invitations, and menus to gain different perspectives on novels and their characters and authors. When I sit down to evaluate my students' final papers, I find myself reading fresh personal narratives that contain valid insight rather than trite, traditional book reviews.

Patricia D. Donaldson, Hershey Middle School, Hershey, Pennsylvania

SYMBOLS IN HAND

After the class read Dickens's *Great Expectations,* I asked each student to bring in a "symbol," an object representative of one of the characters from the book. The following day each student in turn showed an object while the rest of the class made a note of who had brought it, what it was, and what character they thought it represented.

In a class of thirty-four, there was no duplication! Items brought included a stuffed rubber glove with red pen lines to represent Molly's wrists, two five-pound notes given to Pip, white socks with holes in them for Miss Havisham, a piece of dirty, ragged netting for her wedding veil, a clock stopped at 8:40, a cane for Tickler used by Mrs. Joe to "bring Pip up by hand," the convict's file, Mr. Jaggers's top hat, a map of Australia for Magwitch's stay there. The guesses and ensuing discussion were worth far more than a test might have been. The class was excited, interested in each other's guesses, and recovered many details from the novel. I recommend this activity as a follow-up for many novels.

Mary M. Burman, Laramie Junior High School, Laramie, Wyoming

THE MOOD MUSEUM

While discussing the different moods created by Madeleine L'Engle in *A Wrinkle in Time*, I found myself struggling to help my seventh-grade students understand the concept of mood. A discussion ensued about the nature of mood during which the words we used were full of color and action: gray, red, and murky brown; swirls, violence, whirlpool, calm, tornado. When we finished Madeleine L'Engle's book, I decided to assign a project that would enhance our understanding of mood and the following Mood Project was the result.

Students pick any eight of the twelve chapters of *A Wrinkle in Time*, and skim each of those chapters to recall its mood. For each chapter they then create an abstract shape, the color and movement of which reflects the mood of the chapter. Underneath each mood description they write two paragraphs. The first paragraph is a very brief summary of the chapter. The second and more lengthy paragraph defines the mood of the chapter as they see it and explains how their depiction represents that mood.

Originally, I handed posterboard-size paper to each student, suggesting that they divide the sheet into eight equal parts: four on the top half and four on the bottom half (see example below). Most students did so; however, one student chose to make his mood project flow in a circle. He felt that Madeleine L'Engle's method of playing with time deserved a representation other than linear.

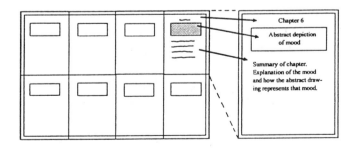

After they have finished their projects, I evaluate them, giving each a written response and discussing it with them if there is time. One day soon after, when they walk into the classroom, all of their projects are displayed—I call it "The Mood Museum." We spend as much time as needed walking around the room looking at all of the projects and asking the artists questions if we have any. (Glasses of apple juice and cheese and crackers add to the atmosphere.)

I have found that students who have difficulty writing, but are artistic, thrive on this assignment. Other students also find themselves stretching during the assignment. It seems to be an effective combination of creative and analytical activity. Whether used with junior high school students in the central city or high school students from the suburbs, I have found this assignment to be a success at eliciting a deeper awareness of the writer's technique and intention, as well as encouraging students to examine a work at more than basic comprehension level.

Jim Rosengarten, Mill Creek School, Philadelphia, Pennsylvania

UPDATING THE BOOK REPORT

What to do about book reports for freshmen? The question kept repeating itself to me as each new year rolled around. After tinkering with book reporting methods, I have finally found a way to offer my students variety and flexibility—I ask for four different types of book reports over the course of the school year.

At the heart of my system is a sincere wish to give my students a wide range of books to choose from. In the first of four quarters, I place only one restriction on students' selections: the books must be novels. In the second quarter, students are asked to read at least one biography or autobiography. A list of "classics" gives students another required book for the third quarter. During that term, students may nominate a classic that the list overlooks. In the fourth quarter, students nominate their favorite books for a "Best of the Year" list, and then each student must read at least one book from the list.

Varying the book selections in this way gives the students shelves of books to choose from, and at the same time helps students avoid getting into a rut where they read only fantasy or only Stephen King novels.

I set aside one day a week, usually Friday, as a "free reading" day. During the period, the students either read or work on their reading reports. While the class is reading or working, I call students to a table in the front of the room for individual conferences. Occasionally, we take trips to the library so they can see where the biographies are shelved, to check out new books, or to hear an enthusiastic book talk given by our librarian.

After students have finished reading a book, they need to make their report. What form the report will take is determined by a sequence. The first book report of each quarter requires a student-teacher conference. In this conference I usually ask about the book's basics: plot, characters, setting. Then I ask questions about students' responses and judgments. As the year progresses, I can make suggestions, note patterns, and generally personalize ideas about reading. I like these informal conferences because both the student and I have a voice in deciding what to talk about. The creative book report must be related in some way to the book they've read. Students can write a poem inspired by the book, write a new chapter or story, build a model of something important in the story such as a ship or a castle, do a painting, write and perform a radio script, or do any other creative spinoff from their book. Many students enjoy the escape from the written word to create an artistic expression of their feelings about a book. The bonus for me is a new supply of projects to put on the bulletin board or in the display case outside the classroom door.

The other two book reports are more typical. The third report is a book review. It follows the normal format of a brief summary, a discussion of key features, and an appraisal. This report is valuable because it involves students in using the higher-order thinking skills of analysis and evaluation.

Finally, the fourth book report is the simplest and shortest. It's a group of responses rather than a report. Students first jot down a précis of the plot, a list of characters, and publication information. Then they respond in short answers to five to seven questions we've brainstormed ahead of time. These questions represent anything students might want to know about a book to help them decide whether or not to read it. Questions might range from "Which did you like best—the characters, the writing style, or the plot?" to "Did you like this book as well as the 'favorite book' you put on the list?" to "Would you read another book by the same author?" If desired, the finished responses can be posted in the classroom to entice prospective readers.

When the students have finished a book report, I record the author and title on a 5" x 8" book card. The book cards help students remember what they have read, and the cards tell me and future teachers what patterns of reading the students have followed. During an individual conference, I may bring up for discussion a book from an earlier quarter. For example, I may ask a student to think about connections between *Grapes of Wrath,* which he or she just finished reading, and *Lord of the Flies,* from the last quarter. The card follows students as they progress to new teachers at the start of each year. At the end of the senior year, the cards make a nice memento of all the books the students read in high school.

I look forward to the reading day each week. I have an opportunity to talk person-to-person with students in a quiet setting. The students and I enjoy the variety of choices for their reports. Best of all, the reading day encourages my freshmen to read widely in books they enjoy.

Kenneth G. Ballinger, Missoula, Montana

NOT ANOTHER BOOK REPORT

I believe strongly in the power of reading and the need for my sixth-grade students to read good books. However, the students groan and, at times, try alternate methods like copying book jackets or rewriting plots. Now, I have happily adapted an alternate method myself, the reading log, which has produced good results. My sixth-grade students are reading and enjoying the process while they learn.

The reading log focuses on time spent reading. Students spend a minimum of ten minutes per day, five days per week, in personal reading. Their choice of reading material is entirely their own and they are not required to finish any work. They choose from books of fiction or nonfiction, magazines, poetry, drama, newspapers, comic books, or any combination of works.

They log in each day, including a complete bibliography the first time a work is begun. They log the time they begin reading, the time they finish, and the total minutes for that day. In addition, for every ten minutes of reading, they must have at least one written reading response.

They have a wide variety of choices for reading responses. They can summarize contents, question passages in any way they wish, predict outcomes, make vocabulary entries, apply what they're reading to their own lives, or write their opinions. The latter two are the most popular options. Students like to write about what they imagine they would do in the same situation. They also like to critique passages that catch their attention—usually, critiquing positively. They write, "I like . . ." and comment on what was said or done, often something that they found humorous.

I evaluate logs on the basis of three criteria: amount of time logged, quality of reading material, and quality of comments.

The results of this process have been both satisfying and encouraging. Many students find that once they really get into a book they don't want to put it down, regardless of log time requirements. Some students enjoy switching reading material by shifting to shorter works like articles and short stories. Most students take more time than the required minimum, and most students seek out high-quality reading material (even if they do so initially only to earn a higher grade). Finally, I feel our goals are more than achieved since there is no doubt that students are reading, and they are reading with a high level of personal involvement. I thoroughly enjoy the time I spend reading student logs.

Frances I. Castle, St. Columba School, San Diego, California

REVIEWING THE BESTSELLERS

Two of the major goals of most middle school and high school English programs are the development of lifelong reading habits and the development of a critical attitude toward the reading of literature. To address these goals, I have started using the following project, which has the added benefits of individualizing instruction and enhancing the process approach to writing. I outline the procedure as follows:

1. Ask students to read two or three book reviews from newspapers or magazines. To help provide students with a variety of approaches, you might want to copy interesting reviews from such sources as *Time, People*, local newspapers, *The New York Times Book Review* section, and so on.

2. After students read several reviews each, begin a discussion of the characteristics of a good review. Ask students, "What do the reviews you read have in common?" or "What elements seem to be most im portant in a review?" As students make suggestions, list them on the chalkboard. Students are likely to note characteristics and features such as plot summary, discussion of themes, evaluative comments, comparisons to similar literary works, comparisons to earlier writings by the same author, and suggestions for what the author could have done differently.

3. Ask students to notice the different ways reviewers begin their pieces. Again, make a list of students' comments. This list might include the following: the use of a quotation, a summary of a dramatic or meaningful scene from the book, a discussion of one of the themes, a question, and others.

4. Hand out copies of a list of recent bestsellers or recommended books. Depending on the reading level of your students, the following book lists might serve as possibilities:

- *The New York Times* "Bestseller" list
- the "Best Books for Young Adults" list (eighty recommended titles) or "Quick Picks for Great Reading" (a list of recommended books for reluctant young adult readers), published in the spring issue of *The Journal of Youth Services in Libraries*
- the "K–12 Bestsellers in the U.S." or "K–12 Bestsellers in Canada" list, published in *The Emergency Librarian*
- the "Reviewer's Choice" list from the September 1990 issue of *English Journal* (p. 97)
- "Young Adult Editor's Choice," a list of recommended titles and annotations, published in the January issue of *Booklist*

Ask students to select a bestseller or recommended book to read. (They'll be responsible for obtaining a copy from the local library.)

5. Give students approximately three weeks from the day they bring their books to class to finish the books. This might include everyday class time for reading or a combination of class time and out-of-class time. Model the activity by selecting and reading a bestseller during the same time period.

6. When students have finished reading, let them meet in groups of three or four and exchange ideas on their books. You might model this task as well by presenting a quick, informal "book chat," mentioning the title and author of your book, your favorite part, your least favorite part, anything that annoyed you or delighted you about the author's writing style, anything you wish the author had done differently, any author or book you were reminded of, and so on. Students then exchange the same type of brief impressions in their groups.

7. Having gained a clearer sense of their own impressions through their group exchanges, students are ready to write a review using the professional models as guides. Remind students to consider their audience while writing. An appropriate audience might be fellow students.

8. After students revise their reviews to their own satisfaction, the finished products may be shared with the class through reading aloud, via a bulletin board display, or by publishing a classroom version of *The New York Times Book Review*. Reviews might also be submitted to the school newspaper.

Most students get a kick out of reading something that's on a bestseller list or highly recommended, and the dialogue between students on published reviews and on their own reviews adds special meaning to this activity. A real literary atmosphere takes over the classroom, in which not only the teacher, but every student, is an expert.

John Barrett, Farmington Public Schools, Farmington, Michigan

EXPLORING CHARACTERS IN *ALL TOGETHER NOW*

It's not surprising that young adult novels can sometimes prompt a stronger response from students than do the time-honored classics of literature. The characters and plots in young adult novels generally parallel people and events in students' own lives; the emotional crises and struggles faced by the protagonists tend to be ones that all adolescents face. Because of students' heightened interest and the degree to which they relate to the characters, young adult novels provide a natural background against which to explore literary concepts such as character development, motivation, and point of view.

Sue Ellen Bridgers's novel *All Together Now* (Knopf, 1979) is a good choice for class reading and closer examination. As in Bridgers's other young adult novels, *Home before Dark* (Bantam, 1985), and *Notes for Another Life* (Knopf, 1981), the characters in *All Together Now* are finely and realistically drawn, the settings are of historical importance, and the plots combine external action with interior, emotional events. The reading level for Bridgers's novels is designated as upper elementary, but, depending on students' ability, the characterization and plot development might be better appreciated by readers in grades eight through ten.

All Together Now focuses on relationships, showing people of various ages reaching out toward companionship and understanding. The novel's main character is twelve-year-old Casey. She is spending the summer with her grandparents because her father is fighting in the Korean War and her mother is holding down two jobs. This is the last summer of her childhood, her last summer to pretend she is a boy and to be left alone to enjoy being a kid. For Casey, the summer's most important figure is her new friend Dwayne, a man of thirty-five whose mental capabilities remain at a small boy's level. In addition to Casey and Dwayne, other characters whose points of view are presented include: Casey's grandmother, Jane; Casey's grandfather, Ben; Jane's best friend, Pansy; Hazard, an old friend of the family; Casey's uncle, Taylor; and Taylor's girlfriend, Gwen. Through glimpses into these characters' thoughts, the reader sees Jane's affection and fears for her granddaughter, sees Taylor sorting out his goals and expectations of life through his relationship with Gwen, and watches Pansy and Hazard move hesitantly from years of familiarity to begin a new relationship.

As students read the novel, the following assignments may help them understand the motivations behind the characters' behavior and relate the fictional characters to their own lives.

1. After you have read the description of Hazard in chapter 2, explain your impression of him. Do you think you will like him? Is he similar to anyone you know? What does Jane think of him?

2. In chapter 2, what is Casey's motivation for letting Dwayne believe she is a boy? Sometimes lies such as this one are called white lies. Write about a time when you told a white lie. Then assume that you were caught in the lie, and write a persuasive letter explaining your rationale for the lie.

3. Using the first person, tell the story of Hazard's life up to where the novel begins, from his point of view. Invent details as necessary.

4. In chapter 8, Dwayne's gift to Casey means a lot to her. Explain why it is so significant. Then write about a time when you received a gift that was of equal importance to you.

5. Pansy and Hazard's honeymoon, described in chapter 10, is a disaster. Could you have predicted that it would be? Contrast their values and expectations using evidence from the text.

6. In chapter 11, Marge blows up at Dwayne. Describe Dwayne's mood and what he is thinking about before, during, and after this scene. What words, phrases, and images are used to convey Dwayne's feelings? Write about a personal experience when you felt the same way Dwayne did after his encounter with Marge.

7. Describe the impression that you have of Gwen when you first meet her in chapter 6. Trace the development of her character in chapters 7, 8, 11, 14, and 15. Is your overall view of Gwen any different by the end of the book? If so, explain what particular details or events alter your first impression of her. Describe what you predict Gwen's future with Taylor will be like.

8. Casey believes the adults have let her down because Dwayne has to spend the night in jail. Write about a time when you, too, had the sense of being let down. Could the situation have been changed? Is there a time when you felt you let someone else down?

9. How do different characters in the novel view Casey? How does Taylor's view of Casey change over the course of the novel? Use passages from the novel to support your opinion.

10. Descriptions of our own family members, including ourselves, would change depending on the point of view. Write a description of yourself or someone else you know very well—a close friend, a brother or sister, or even a pet—from your own viewpoint. Then write a detailed description of the same individual, seen through someone else's eyes.

11. After reading the description of the car race in chapter 6, write about a similar event or activity that you have been part of or have witnessed. Choose your verbs and adjectives carefully to give your description a sense of movement and excitement.

12. By the conclusion of the novel, Casey feels that she has learned much about responsibility and love. Describe the changes she has gone through and the results of those changes. Find specific passages that illustrate what, in your opinion, are significant learning experiences for Casey.

Rhoda Maxwell, University of Wisconsin–Eau Claire

IF YOU CAN'T BEAT 'EM, JOIN 'EM

Using the Romance Series to Confront
Gender Stereotypes

I drool over young adult literature. When I see a new book by Chris Crutcher or Cynthia Voigt, I snatch it off the store shelf and buy it. When I see an advertisement that announces that Gary Paulsen or Sue Ellen Bridgers or Walter Dean Myers has a new book out, I call up my local bookstore and order it. When I go to the fall convention of the National Conference of Teachers of English, I bring only one extra suitcase so I won't overdo it at the book exhibits and buy more books than I can carry to the airplane.

Because I know the field of young adult literature well and know how much good writing there is in this field and because I have over 800 novels in my classroom that I happily share with my students, it pains me when students ask me for books like *Sweet Valley High* or *Sweet Dreams*—the romance series.

Besides their being simplistic and of mediocre writing quality, an even greater concern I have about these novels is that the girls who read these books will measure themselves against the girls shown in the books. The "normal" girls in the books are usually very good-looking: Elizabeth and her twin Jessica in *Deceptions* (Sweet Valley High #14) are "spectacular, with the all-American good looks that made them the envy of every other girl in Sweet Valley" (p. 3). Being told that one is pretty is considered the highest compliment.

I also worry that girls might take seriously the way females are divided into "admirable" and "not-admirable" people. In the same book, Jessica is shown as rather conniving and shallow mainly because she is described as selfish. Elizabeth, on the other hand, is elevated because she worries about other people. Of course, the same standards do not appear to apply to males, who are all allowed to think mainly of themselves. Girls are more readily condemned in these novels if they make mistakes and are not allowed the "boys-will-be-boys" maxim that excuses males from mistakes. I worry that, if my female students buy into these books, they will be too harsh on themselves.

I have talked to girls about the appeal of reading these books. I have also talked to two worried parents whose daughters have read widely in many genres but have also read every number in the romance series. What I have found out surprises me. I thought that girls were only reading these books because they were desperate to have boys in their lives. But I have found out that girls often read these books for comfort when they are upset. There is a sameness in each book that they can count on. They feel safe when they read these books because doing so takes them away from whatever is going on in their lives. The most serious problem in these books is usually how to catch and keep a boy. There are no parents arguing, no one demanding they do anything, no one challenging their view of the world. Everyone is pretty much the same in these books. Everything at home gets done magically. Crime and violence do not exist. This predictability seems to be soothing to the readers.

The soothing effect of these books was made clear to me when my own twelve-year-old daughter went through Nancy Drew books in big gulps. Not only did she read every one, but, when something was bothering her, she would reread them again and again. That experience suggested to me the idea that these books might be escapes for their readers. I found out that similar patterns existed when I questioned two of my friends who were offended and upset that their daughters read books in the *Sweet Valley High* series. They too had observed that their daughters read these books over and over again, apparently finding comfort in reading them.

Although reading the romance series for escape seems harmless enough, I still prefer to hide them at the back of my book racks at school, hoping students will find something else before they come to them. Experience has taught me that bad-mouthing these books or chiding students for reading them does not work. These books appeal to teens. So instead of ignoring them or trying to subvert their appeal, I decided I might instead learn to use these books in ways that can provoke thought and encourage readers to look closely at what these novels really say, especially about male and female roles By helping students become conscious of such issues as the gender expectations shown in the books, I can help them think about their own values and expectations for males and females.

The major theme that appears to run throughout the romance series is the girls' desire to be accepted, usually by a member of the opposite sex. This desire to be accepted should not come as a surprise to us, since we are dealing with young teens who are trying to figure out who they are and how they can get people to like them.

Although we cannot expect to take readers from Sweet Valley High (where girls who have boyfriends have a higher status) to a heightened awareness of sexism in one bound, using these books and raising and discussing the issues in them is certainly a beginning. Since approaching any issue in preachy ways won't get students to look closely at the issue, it is advisable to start out gently and indirectly.

For students who are planning to read these books, the teacher could construct a series of questions and ask these students before they begin reading to discuss the questions with those who have already read books in the series. Such questions might include:

- What do you look for in a friend?
- What do you think makes you a good friend?
- Are there differences in the ways boys and girls are judged? Explain.
- What do you think appearance tells you about someone?
- If people judged you on your appearance, what might they conclude about you?
- What kind of people would you rather not be friends with?
- Is it important to you whether or not your friends are involved in school activities and/or athletics? Explain.
- What activities or interests in school bring status or importance to boys? To girls?
- How might people your age react if a male wanted to be a ballet dancer?
- How might people your age react if a female wanted to be a football player?

It is difficult to discuss gender issues with preteens and young teens because they are still grappling with their own sexuality. So in my classes I try to illustrate the adverse effects of gender stereotyping on both males and females: gender stereotyping limits choices and opportunities. Both boys and girls can be hurt by gender expectations. When students start to understand the negative effects of such stereotyping, they are usually a bit more willing to discuss gender issues. After reading these very short novels, students might discuss why these books appeal to teens and what information is contained in them.

- How do these books show "normal" behavior in high school?
- What is usually involved in a relationship?
- What do males expect of females in a relationship? What do females expect of males?
- When females are involved in relationships, how are they viewed?
- When males are involved in relationships, how are they viewed?
- How are males and females shown acting around the opposite sex?
- Which portrayals of males and females seem realistic? Unrealistic?

The next step may be to get students talking about and recognizing some of the sexism in these books. Teachers can select sample activities from the list below, perhaps asking students who read these books to respond to a few of the questions in place of the more traditional book report that only asks students to report on what is in the book, not question it.

- List words used to describe male and female characters. Compare them.
- List what males and females are shown doing in the story. Look at the verbs that describe what they are doing.
- Compare the way female appearance is described with the way male appearance is described. What do such descriptions say about what we expect of males and females?
- What are males shown doing in the novel that results in disapproval of them? What are females shown doing in the novel that results in disapproval of them?
- How are fathers portrayed? What are they shown doing? What is expected of them? What are they criticized for? What about mothers?
- Who seems to have the power in the teen relationships shown? Do you believe there should be differences in male and female behavior? What should they be?
- Compare males and females in the novels in terms of the following personality characteristics: active/passive; stable/unstable; courageous/afraid; risk-taker/complier; aggressive/non-aggressive; challenging/obedient; low need to have friends/ high need to have friends; competitive/nurturing. What are males criticized for? What are females criticized for?
- What personality characteristics are valued for males? What personality characteristics are valued for females?
- How does the author characterize females in contrast to males? What is primarily used to show what kind of person the character is? Speech? Appearance? Actions? What others say about them?
- What characters seem to have the most interesting plans for the future?
- Who seems to be the most intelligent? the most sensitive? the most emotional?

Once students start to look at these romance series through the lens of gender expectations, they might still read these series just as much—but there is a chance that they might become aware of both how sexist the series is and how these novels promote the idea that involvement in a traditional romantic relationship is the answer to any girl's problem. Generally, with young girls, the process of questioning the way females are portrayed in the books they read is a bit threatening. They want to avoid being labeled as "feminists," since in middle school and high school they associate the term with females who are not accepted by males because they appear too independent. So this questioning process may be slow, but, over a period of time, with gentle urging from the teacher, romance-series readers can learn to be more objective about what they read. Thus, since many of our female students have a natural attraction to the romance series either as a way of finding solace in an increasingly demanding world or as a way to reassure themselves of happy endings, we as teachers need to use this interest as an opening instead of fighting the losing battle of warning students against reading them.

Diana Mitchell, Sexton High School, Lansing, Michigan

4 EMPHASIS: CREATING COMMUNITIES OF READERS

THE READING INVENTORY: A NEW TWIST

For years I've relied on a reading inventory in getting to know my students and their interests. Occasionally I've referred them to their completed inventories when they've complained. "I don't know what to read." Only recently, however, have I glimpsed the possibilities an inventory offers.

Let me begin with twenty typical inventory questions.

1. What are three questions to which you'd like the answer?
2. Have you ever wondered how something works? Name a mechanism or object you'd like to know more about.
3. What is your favorite after-school activity?
4. List three favorite weekend activities.
5. What two places would you most like to visit?
6. When you are alone, how do you occupy your time?
7. If you could have three wishes (you can't wish for more wishes), what would they be?
8. What do you dislike about school?
9. If you could talk to any three people in the world, living or dead, who would they be?
10. If you could live at any time in history—past, present, or future—what time would you choose? Be specific.
11. When you are thirty years old, what do you think you will be doing for a living?
12. If you had $1000, how would you spend it?
13. Name the skill you possess of which you are most proud.
14. What skill would you most like to improve?
15. List three things you hope to accomplish before you die.
16. If you could ask anybody in the whole world any question, who would you ask and what would the question be?
17. Where (aside from the school) is the last place on earth you'd like to be right now and why?

18. Name something you are now or once were terrified by.
19. Since you have to study history, which period would you choose to study?
20. If you were to recommend a book to a friend, what book would you recommend and why?

I ask students to respond in complete sentences, to vary sentence structure, and to answer honestly and thoroughly. When inventories are complete, students convert fifteen of their answers into subject or topic areas. I get them started with examples from my answers to the inventory. For instance:

> *Inventory question*: What is your favorite after-school activity?
> *Answer*: After school, I enjoy taking a nap.
> *Related subject or topic areas*: fatigue (exhaustion), dreams, health, sleep research (REM sleep)

Developing these topics requires creative brainstorming and a lot of help from each other, but when each student has fifteen lists of topics, we discuss the concept of "too broad/too narrow." Together we try to establish realistic, workable topics, but we don't always succeed.

Next, student go to the library to locate books, articles, and pamphlets related to their topics. They record titles and call numbers and keep this list along with their completed inventories and topic lists in individual folders.

These inventories, as always, help me learn about my students, and they gain some information about me because I post my responses to the inventory. Students have had a useful introduction to the library, and I have been able to asses how well they write sentences—an important piece of information early in the semester. I also develop a book list around student interests that we use for required reading assignments throughout the year. In addition, I have access to a valuable source for composition and discussion topics. And finally, students have become aware of the problems in choosing and developing topics. They quickly learn which subjects are too broad and which too narrow, for there are too many books to choose from for the first and too few or none at all for the second.

Robin Jackson, Mahomet-Seymour Junior High School, Mahomet, Illinois

"IS THIS A GOOD BOOK?"

"Is this a good book?"
"Do you think I'd like this one?"
"This has a pretty cover. Is it good?"

These are typical questions that I hear students repeat as they stand at the free-choice bookshelf. To eliminate this game of twenty questions during silent sustained reading, I have devised a way to help students decide which book to read, with just a simple glance.

The following method is a fast, efficient way to see peer responses to books in question. Simply stick a library book pocket on the inside front cover of all in-class, personal choice novels. Inside this pocket, place a 3" × 5" index card with sections titled *Name* and *Comments*.

After students have completed reading a novel, they can share their opinions of this book with others, but in a silent way. First, students sign their names on the index card. Next, the students draw a happy face or a sad face to the right of their name. Finally, students write a phrase or a short sentence indicating reasons for liking or disliking the novel. I caution students to be specific without giving away too much about the story—especially the ending. Here are some typical examples:

Name	Comments
(for Gary Paulsen's *The Island*) Maria C.	Great book. It made me want to find my own island and write about *me*.
(for Robert Cormier's *The Chocolate War*) Damien J.	This book makes you think, but it has some bad language and is pretty violent at the end.

(for Paula Danziger's *The Divorce Express*) Darlene M.

Phoebe, she just thinks everything's going okay till her mom decides to get married to Duane. Phoebe and Rose are just like my friends. This was a fun book.

(for Christopher Pike's *Die Softly*) Van N.

It's complicated. I had to read it twice over to understand it, but it was worth the trouble. The ending was a really big surprise.

With this method, less silent reading time is wasted on looking for a new book. Now, students can thumb through the shelved books and find not only what the publisher has to say about a particular novel, but what their peers think, also.

This method provides a quick evaluation for the prospective reader. At the same time, the individual who responded to the book is provided with a feeling of satisfaction as a result of someone respecting his or her opinion.

Jami L. Smith, Bedford, Texas

BOOK-OF-THE-MONTH CLUB

Tap into what students do best: talk. The halls ring with their chatter about boy-girl relationships, clothes, sports, gossip of all kinds, but to get them talking about books challenges most of us who teach secondary students. Book groups or clubs—a term one student used in her response journal last year ("I've never been in a book club before, and I love it.") have proved successful in my eighth- and ninth-grade general English classrooms.

Students select a book each month to read outside of class. I provide a booklist and include a few notes on each book. I do put some books recommended by others on the list; I tell the students that I have not read them but also explain what I know about them. Students may recommend titles for the booklist too; I ask for student suggestions in advance and ask that students provide a copy of the book for me to review.

At first, the groups form around interest in a particular title, availability of the book, and perhaps most importantly, people with whom they want to work. Students are given class time once a week to plan how much they will read during the week and to discuss the book.

To prepare for the meetings, students write questions about the reading, find quotes they like, or note themes they would like to discuss. At times we divide the class time in half, the last half of the period for discussion and the first half for a written response in their journals.

At the end of the month, students share their books in a variety of ways. Last month, I asked the students to present a visual and written response for their classmates and another response persuading their parents to read the book. A group who read *Alive: The Story of the Andes Survivors* (Avon, 1979) by Piers Paul Read did a video of the plane crash, included discussions among the survivors, and showed them eating the bodies of the dead. For their parents, they created a poster of the mountain, marking the landing site and other places of interest, including the various routes the survivors took while seeking a way off the mountain.

Both the students and I look forward to meeting dates. The students say that they feel free to ask questions of group members, questions they would feel silly asking in class. Many have also mentioned that they get different perspectives on the book, and most of all, they love working with their friends.

Rachel Reinhard, Upper Arlington High School, Columbus, Ohio

PROJECT "SIBLING LITERACY"

"Why don't you get one of the books from over there? These are for little kids."

"But I love The Tailypo. *It's my favorite book."*

This was an exchange I had with Robert, a sixth-grade student who had reading problems. But it was far from uncommon; in fact, I found myself continually rerouting these "reluctant readers" toward the age-appropriate library books. Still, I could not forget the pride of ownership and show of confidence these students exhibited when given an opportunity to revisit their favorite picture books.

About this time I was also studying various theories concerning literacy acquisition. I encountered study after study that indicated reading to preschool children positively affects their literacy development. In *Becoming a Nation of Readers* (National Academy of Education, 1985), the commission concluded, "The single most important activity for building the knowledge required for eventual success in reading is reading aloud to children." But it is clear, within the context of today's societal trends and pressures, that far too many youngsters haven't interacted with stories and print in books before they enter school. It finally dawned on me that my sixth-grade students, given their love and enthusiasm for picture books, were a valuable resource. Project Sibling Literacy involved these students, along with their parents, in furthering the literacy development of some young children.

I began by giving students an overview of the project and asking for volunteers. Obviously, access to a child, whether a sibling, relative, or a neighbor, was a prerequisite. The participants agreed to read aloud to their "partners" at least twice each week and to attend occasional after-school meetings. The students chose books from my collection or from the public library. A camera and tape recorder were also available for participants to take home. I requested photos of their book-sharing experiences, generally taken by a parent. I kept one photo and displayed it with others on bulletin boards, and gave the other to the student to share with parents and partners. We listened to some of the audio recordings of reading sessions together, laughing at humorous incidents and examining how these are really informal teaching/learning sessions. We enjoyed snacks or pizza at these after-school meetings, and had a big reward party for students who participated all year.

I sent a letter home to the parents of all participants, explaining the program and encouraging them to become actively involved. Obviously, they were invited to join in all the book-sharing sessions. They were asked to view at home a 13-minute videotape, distributed by the International Reading Association, which provides pointers on how to read to young children and a convincing presentation of its beneficial effects. Each was also asked to initial the student's record sheet, confirming that the reading sessions did take place. Lastly, near the end of the year, a letter to parents encouraged them to take both the sixth grader and the young child to a public library regularly and continue the family reading sessions.

I conducted no formal evaluation of the effects of Project Sibling Literacy. I did, however, hear about how some children responded. I heard some of my students complaining that their young brother or sister "bugged" them every night to read this or that book to them. Others told me their partners had the books memorized. I could not have hoped for better results.

Parents also responded positively to the project. Many of them told me about becoming more involved in reading to the younger siblings after they saw how much they enjoyed the stories. Parents also told me about improved relationships between siblings as they took part in the book-sharing sessions. Some informed me that they saw their older child doing more independent reading as the year progressed, also. Again, all of this was good news.

The "teachers" in this project learned as well. They learned to see themselves as real readers, with authentic audiences. As they read to their partners and discussed their sessions with other participants, they exhibited a heightened awareness that reading, writing, and speaking are developmental, and they, too, could improve their skills with practice.

In the end, I benefitted most from this project. I learned to ask the next sixth grader with an affinity for picture books, "Do you have a younger brother or sister?" rather than, "Don't you know these are for little kids?"

Ramey Haddican, Hodges Bend Middle School, Houston, Texas

PROMOTING RECREATIONAL READING

I became concerned when I discovered that many—too many!—of my college prep freshmen and sophomores did not read for entertainment. This limited their vocabulary and spelling skills, as well as their experience with ideas and cultural information. To help remedy this, I developed a series of assignments intended to promote recreational reading.

I started out by requiring students to devote a set amount of time each week to independent reading projects. I gave them the following instructions:

> For the first quarter—beginning this week!—each student will be required to read for one hour a week, in addition to other English class homework assignments. You will have complete freedom of choice with regard to what you read; any book or magazine is acceptable as long as it is not required reading for another class.
>
> No book report or project will be required as proof that the reading has been completed. Instead, each student will ask a parent or guardian to sign a reading record certifying that the one hour's reading has been completed. The sheet for this quarter is attached to this memo. Keep this sheet somewhere safe; your reading grade for the first quarter depends upon the completion of the sheet and its being returned to me on time. This assignment will be weighted as a test.

Students received a reading log similar to the following:

Reading Log: Quarter I
Student: _____ Hour: _____
The parent's signature below certifies that to his or her knowledge the student read an unassigned book or magazine for one hour during the week.

Week	Book or Magazine	Parent's Signature
1		
2		
3		
4		
5		
6		
7		
8		

Date Due:

My next project was to initiate an optional book discussion group for students and parents. I sent out an invitational letter that began as follows:

I, like all English teachers, love to read. My idea of the perfect Saturday is to curl up in a corner somewhere with a good novel and read the whole thing uninterrupted. But as much as I love reading for myself, I love it more when I have a chance to share my reactions with other people who have read the same book. I believe that most people share that feeling; I believe that most people enjoy a book even more when they have a chance to share it with someone else. Toward that end, I would like to invite parents and students together to participate in a monthly reading and discussion group.

The remainder of my letter outlined the mechanics of the group. We would meet at school one evening a month for an hour and a half. At the end of each meeting, we would select the book to be discussed at the following session. Each family would have to supply its own books, but we would try to select titles readily available in the local libraries. I cautioned those participating to be patient if the selection was not a title for which they had voted; eventually their choice would be selected. Most of all, I emphasized that I felt parents and students alike would enjoy hearing each other's opinions about a book and that we would all learn from each other.

For the first month, I suggested *The Color Purple* by Alice Walker, *The Phantom of the Opera* by Gaston Leroux, *A Brief History of Time* by Stephen J. Hawking, and *Out of Africa* by Isak Dinesen. Twelve families responded to my invitation, and we decided to read *The Phantom of the Opera* by an overwhelming majority. The uncontested choice for the second month was Russell Baker's *Growing Up*. The response to the reading group was so enthusiastic that I hope to open up the group to all freshmen students, and perhaps even invite schoolwide participation.

As a final activity to promote recreational reading, my ninth-grade students will be reading Newbury and Caldecott award winning books—to students at a nearby elementary school. Students will work in groups to develop ten- to fifteen-minute oral presentations based on the books they select. They will prepare visual aids to augment their presentations, in which they will either read or act out a segment from the book. The object will be to encourage the younger students to read the particular book, and hopefully my students will enjoy these books as well.

Carolyn P. Henly, Webster Groves High School, Webster Groves, Missouri

STUDENT-SUGGESTED MULTICULTURAL READINGS

I teach in a high school in which thirty-eight nationalities are represented. I devised the following multicultural reading and review project for a class of youngsters from fifteen different countries and states. This project gives students an experience recommending books that is less like a traditional book report and more like the way readers suggest books to one another. Students have a stronger motive for reading and a more flexible format for their recommendations of books to their peers. And the project reaches more students than just those who read and recommend books—the finished student reviews of multicultural fiction and nonfiction become library resources for both school and public.

First, I asked students to find and read a book (autobiography, biography, fiction, or travel) by an author representative of their individual culture or ethnic background. The school librarian and I helped as needed. Students had some time in class to read, but completed most of the reading on their own time.

A wide range of authors and genres was represented among the final selections. Students from the Caribbean and South America had read histories and travel books about Guyana and Jamaica, as well as biographies of Simón Bolívar, José Feliciano, and Diego Rivera. Students whose grandparents or great-grandparents had lived in the American South had read *The Adventures of Huckleberry Finn, The Adventures of Tom Sawyer,* Zora Neale Hurston's *Their Eyes Were Watching God,* Maya Angelou's *I Know Why the Caged Bird Sings,* and John Howard Griffin's *Black Like Me.* Other students had chosen cookbooks from the countries of their origin, and went so far as to prepare traditional dishes and describe the holidays or special occasions on which they were enjoyed.

In class discussion, students revealed some of the things they found out through their reading and noted struggles each successful person had in the times in which he or she lived. After reading about Maya Angelou's life, Mayra said, "I thought having children was the answer to today's teenagers who don't feel loved. Now I understand how much more of a problem having children too young is." Ricardo said, "I learned that there were black poets like Langston Hughes and Mari Evans who wrote about their feelings."

In drafting their reviews, students used as models book review sections of *The New York Times.* Many students had jotted down comments and reactions as they read and were able to incorporate these details into their recommendations.

We talked in class about the type of information found in book reviews; students noted that professionally written book reviews usually included enough of a synopsis of the story to capture readers' interest. We also brainstormed factors that influence whether someone would read a particular book. Suggestions included familiarity with the author, attractiveness of the cover, interest in the subject matter, inspirational value, and length. When students were ready, they drafted, revised, and edited their reviews in the word-processing laboratory.

A small group of students had indicated interest in learning desktop publishing techniques; I met with them before school and during lunch periods to show them how to position the book reviews on the page and insert graphics into the text. With these skills, they were able to prepare our booklet of student-suggested multicultural readings for the school and public libraries.

We reproduced, collated, and assembled the booklets, giving each member of the class a copy, and left about two hundred in the school library to let other students know what their peers enjoyed reading and why.

This project enabled the students in my class to expand their literary canon far more than I could have done by covering only one or two authors. In their evaluations of the project, students made other benefits apparent as well: they recognized that they had learned about literature and about their own cultural backgrounds and felt that they had learned from one another.

Carol Gladstone, James Monroe High School, Bronx, New York

EXPLORING PREJUDICE IN YOUNG ADULT LITERATURE
Through Drama and Role Play

Young adult literature provides rich literary material for exploring issues and dilemmas of the human experience as perceived by the young. The dramatization of cultural pluralism is one of the major roles this literature can play. The adolescent years are timely years for dealing with issues of discrimination, prejudice, and cultural differences since adolescents often perceive themselves as a "culture" apart from the mainstream. Thus, authors of young adult fiction who deal with themes of diversity in race, religion, gender, or class can touch young readers in a profound way.

But these matters are difficult ones, fraught with the potential to unleash prejudices inherited by the young from their elders. Merely reading and discussing cultural, ethnic, and racial issues in the stories of such authors as Virginia Hamilton, Mildred Taylor, J. Okada, Rosa Guy, and others may only affect attitudes on one level. Often these problems are dealt with in ways that allow students to remain removed from the human conflicts involved—literature is read, the problems discussed, the issues abstracted. An empathetic understanding of the complexities and human feelings involved is difficult to achieve. Dramatization or "living through" the thoughts, feelings, and experiences of the characters can provide students with a deeper, more immediate experience. Through dramatics, teachers can help their students connect with sensitive, complicated human issues with a sense of empathy.

ROLL OF THUNDER, HEAR MY CRY

There are many young adult books, stories, and poems that deal with cultural diversity and with young people sorting through and confronting the issue of being "different" of finding their place in a sometimes confusing and diverse world. However, drama as a teaching tool is often most effective when a single, powerful stimulus is used. Mildred Taylor's beautifully crafted novel, *Roll of Thunder, Hear My Cry*, provides such a stimulus. It provides an authentic view of black culture as experienced from the inside.

Set in Mississippi in 1933, the story covers twelve turbulent months in the life of the Logans, a black land-owning family. The narrator is Cassie Logan, an independent-minded, nine-year-old girl who questions the social situation that requires her to be subservient to the local white families—even to the point of accepting physical assault by Charlie Simms, for whose daughter Cassie refused to give way on the sidewalk. The Logans had bought their land during the Reconstruction period after the Civil War, but the original owners, the Grangers, are attempting to get it back by fair means or foul. A number of incidents, including the firing of Mary Logan (a progressive teacher) by the white school board, depict the difficulties and apparent powerlessness of the black population who, in this locale, are mainly sharecroppers.

When the involvement of the Wallaces (the white owners of the local store) in the brutal kerosene burning of three black men goes unpunished, the Logans organize a boycott of the Wallace store. Feelings and tensions run high. When T.J. Avery, the bragging and troubled black teenage friend of the Logan boys, is involved in a robbery that leads to murder, he is hunted down. His two white partners in the robbery hypocritically take a leading role in the manhunt. Seeing that a lynching is imminent, David Logan sets fire to his own cotton crop during a fierce thunder and lightning storm. The Grangers, in order to save their adjoining property, divert their fellow whites to join the effort to put out the fire. The book ends with T.J. captured by the law and facing a probable death sentence. Cassie, who has always disliked T.J., weeps for him and for the land and for a trusting innocence that will never again be hers.

USING DRAMA TO EXPLORE DIVERSITY

To demonstrate the potential for using drama to explore cultural diversity, the following drama-based lesson is offered. The lesson, which has been used effectively with English teachers-in-training, in-service teachers, and high school students, is designed to take students through a sequence of drama activities that explore racial prejudice as reflected in Taylor's novel. Using techniques of role play, improvisation, "hot seating," and tableau (freeze frame), students respond to the motives, feelings, and events depicted in several of the novel's scenes.

Focus: Experiences in Prejudice

Objectives
- To give students an opportunity to adopt different cultural perspectives and to respond to the conflicts involved through negotiation "in-role."
- To encourage students to read quality young adult literature that illuminates the conflicts and joys of cultural diversity.
- To provide students with another tool for engaging a piece of literature.

Procedures
Activity 1: "The Warm Up"
(Pair Work/Whole Group)
When using drama to deal with a powerful issue such as racial prejudice, students should first start with an activity that provides them with a situation drawn from their own lives that relates to, or is analogous to the issue.

- *Teacher:* "I'd like you to search your storehouse of memories/experiences (childhood to the present) and try to fix on a time (moment/event) in your life when your ideas about something or someone were abruptly changed—a time when your assumptions about 'how things are' were jolted. This may have been a pleasant or unpleasant awakening. An example from childhood might be the first time you realized there was no Santa Claus." (Vocabulary/examples can be adjusted to suit the class.) "Think for a few moments; jot it down briefly in your journal; then turn to a partner and just talk about it."
- *Students:* They think, write briefly; then dialogue and share in pairs for 3–4 minutes.
- *Whole Group:* Debrief and probe their feelings about the various experiences.

Activity 2: "Extrapolating a Scene from the Novel"
(Improvisation/Role Play)
After reading and reviewing the early scenes (or reading the summary, which presents a skeleton of the story), the students are invited to participate more fully by stepping into one of the key events and improvising the reaction of the fictional community to the event. This improvised "scene" goes beyond the

actions of the novel. In effect, it creates a new scene, one that the author did not include.

- *Teacher:* (Sets up the next situation) "A pivotal event in the story is, of course, the burning with kerosene of Mr. Berry, a black share-cropper and his nephews. This vicious attack is led by Mr. Wallace, the white owner of the town store. One of the nephews has already died. It is a day or two later; tensions are high; there is much talk about the incident; rumors are flying, but no legal action has taken place.

    "I'd like you to pair up. One of you will be 'A'—the other 'B'. Quickly decide. A's, you are a member of the community who was away when the burning occurred. You've just returned and want to know what's happened. You are a gossipy, instigating type. B's, you are a neighbor who was in town and you 'know something.' "

    The teacher then gives the following directions: "Before you role-play a conversation with your partner, I'd like to divide the entire class into two sections. This half of the A/B pairs are white members of the community; this half are black members of the community. Think about who you are for a moment. Then begin."

- *Students:* In role, students engage their partners in conversation for 2–4 minutes.

    As the students role-play the conversation, the teacher circulates, paying close attention to how the students are handling the dialogue, gently keeping them "in role." After a few minutes, the teacher may want to stop the drama momentarily to "eavesdrop" on a particular conversation, asking the rest of the class to listen while this particular dialogue goes on. It is important to be selective in eavesdropping. It is not essential for all students to hear all conversations. Indeed, the teacher may decide that it is better at this point to leave all conversations "private." But if one or two dialogues seem particularly pointed or illuminate the issue well (and these students seem willing), then the teacher might spotlight some of the role play.

- *Debriefing:* It is essential to allow students to express their feelings after engaging in such potentially powerful role play. They need to reflect on and analyze a bit as a whole group what has occurred. The teacher can prompt that response with brief questions such as "Was it difficult or easy for you to do this? How did you feel in your role? Were your partner's questions/responses realistic? What kinds of things did you talk about? What attitudes could you detect in the tone your partner was using?"

Activity 3: "A Quiet Reflection"
(Whole Group)

For this activity, the students sit in a circle and listen as the teacher reviews another poignant scene from the novel. She reminds them that the Logan children have not been told of the specifics about the burning, although they have picked up bits and pieces of information through overhearing the adults talk. They have been strictly forbidden to go near the Wallace store. But Cassie and her brothers disobey, and with their friends they hang around the store. When their mother finds out, instead of punishing them, she decides it's time for Cassie and her brothers to see the brutal consequences of the assault. She takes them to the Berry cabin to bring the family food.

At this point, the teacher asks the students to close their eyes and to listen as she reads this passage from the novel:

> "Daddy, who you s'pose done come to see 'bout us?"
>
> There was no recognizable answer, only an inhuman guttural wheezing. But Mrs. Berry seemed to accept it and went on. "Miz Logan and her babies. Ain't that somethin'?" She took a sheet from a nearby table. "Gots to cover him," she explained. "He can't hardly stand to have nothin' touch him." When she was visible again, she picked up a candle stump and felt around a table for matches. "He can't speak no more. The fire burned him too bad. But he understands all right." Finding the matches, she lit the candle and turned once more to the corner.
>
> A still form lay there staring at us with glittering eyes. The face had no nose, and the head no hair; the skin was scarred, burned, and the lips were wizened black, like charcoal. As the wheezing sound echoed from the opening that was a mouth, Mama said, "Say good morning to Mrs. Berry's husband, children." (Taylor, pp. 73–74)

The teacher stops, waits, and quietly asks the students to think and absorb this scene. After a moment or so, the teacher asks each student to go around the circle and speak a single word or phrase that comes to mind or heart from hearing this passage. The teacher may want to jot down the words on a piece of paper as they are spoken; later these words and phrases could become the basis for writing a poem. All words spoken must be accepted, whether angry or compassionate. After the circle of words is completed, students should be allowed to talk freely about their feelings.

Activity 4: "The Cover Up"
(Secret Meeting Format—Hot Seating/Teacher-in-Role)

Once again, the teacher creates a situation that did not take place in the novel, but one that is consistent with the author's depiction of plot and character. It is important for the teacher to take an active role in the drama here, perhaps portraying the character, Mr. Jamison, the white lawyer who has been sympathetic to the plight of the Logans and the black sharecroppers, or perhaps portraying Jeremy, the shy, secretive white boy who admires the Logan family and hangs around them as much as he can. If some students have completed the novel, they could be "plants" at this secret meeting, perhaps taking on the role of Mr. Wallace or Mr. Simms. The other class members improvise their roles as members of the white community.

- *Teacher:* The teacher leads in: "It is obvious that some members of the white community are involved in a coverup of the burning incident. No legal action has taken place yet, but many are nervous. There is a rumor circulating that little Jeremy saw the whole thing that night while he was hiding up a tree. Everyone knows that he's always hanging around the black kids. What if he tells? A secret meeting is about to take place at the Wallace store—Mr. Wallace, Mr. Simms (Jeremy's father), a reluctant and scared Jeremy, and other members of the white community are there. Jeremy is being badgered with questions as Mr. Jamison walks in. (Teacher in role as Mr. Jamison sets the tone.) "You folks don't mind my dropping by, now do you? Hi there, Jeremy. What you here fo' boy?"
- *Whole Group:* The group takes it from there and the scene unfolds.
- *CAUTION:* This open-ended format is not for everyone. Not all students can handle such volatile drama. Not all teachers will feel comfortable in this role.

Activity 5: "Standing Up For Our Beliefs"
(A Tableau)

The teacher recaps: "We began these activities by searching our memories for a moment in time that shook our values—a frightening, but revealing moment. Cassie has been experiencing this in a big way throughout this book. She's bright and free-spirited, and just learning that the white world expects her to show deference and be submissive. She has to decide what to do about the white girl, Lillian Jean, her supposed friend, who allowed her to be shoved down on the sidewalk and be humiliated. Confused, she turns to her father for advice. Listen to David Logan trying to explain a world of injustice to his 9-year-old daughter":

> "Cassie, there'll be a whole lot of things you ain't gonna wanna do but you'll have to do in this life just so you can survive . . . .
>
> "But there are other things, Cassie, that if I'd let be, they'd eat away at me and destroy me in the end. And it's the same with you, baby. There are things you can't back down on, things you gotta

take a stand on. But it's up to you to decide what them things are. You have to demand respect in this world, ain't nobody gonna hand it to you. How you carry yourself, what you stand for—that's how you gain respect. But, little one, ain't nobody's respect worth more than your own. You understand that?" (Taylor, pp. 133–134)

- *Teacher:* "In groups of 3 or 4, I'd like you to devise a still picture, a visual image to capture the essence of David Logan's message. This picture could be a realistic portrayal (people) or an abstract, symbolic portrayal. The theme of this frozen picture should be: "Standing Up For What You Believe Is Right."
- *Students:* Given 7–8 minutes, the students plan how they could depict this idea. Should they be people in an actual scene from life? (coming to the rescue of a mugging victim perhaps), or could they portray abstract qualities like justice or injustice in a symbolic struggle?

Each group then takes a turn and forms its tableau for 30 seconds or so. The rest of the class may comment on what they think they see in this depiction.

If appropriate, the teacher or a student may want to tap the shoulder of one member of the tableau and allow that person to speak in role—what are his/her thoughts; what emotions are being felt?

- *Debrief:* After each group has presented its tableau, discussion and reflection should follow. What range of situations were presented? What feelings did students experience in portraying the theme? How does one decide when it is time to stand up for one's beliefs? How does one know when it is more important to remain silent? What would you do about Lillian Jean if you were Cassie?

All of the preceding activities are designed to help students connect with sensitive, complicated human issues; not all students will be comfortable with such activities. Techniques like improvisation, role-reversal, and hot-seating can be volatile when dealing with cultural, ethnic, racial, or other social issues that tap the core of our individual value systems and awaken our own latent biases. Working through the screen of a fine work of literature can soften the sting without removing the impact. The key to working successfully with dramatics is the establishment of a classroom atmosphere of trust and respect. Students should never be forced to "perform." Classroom drama is not theatre; it is a way to respond to and explore the lives, situations, struggles, and decisions of young people as portrayed in the best of young adult literature. It is a way to make that literature a learning tool for one's own life.

WORKS CITED

Bontempo, B., and R. Jerome. "Exploring Diversity in Adolescent Literature." Workshop Presentation, National Council of Teachers of English Annual Convention, Baltimore, Maryland, November 19, 1989.

Taylor, Mildred D. *Roll Of Thunder, Hear My Cry*. Bantam Books, 1989.

Barbara T. Bontempo, SUNY College, Buffalo, New York

SHORT STORY SEMINARS

Tired of the old approach? You know—questions and answers to short stories followed by a test? What follows is a three-step approach to weekly short story seminars which can be adapted for any grade level.

First, I hand out short story texts to groups of three and give the students several classes to read and then select a story for their group.

After the groups have signed up for a story of their choice, I ask them to do the following:

Prepare a *Critical* presentation on the story, including characterization, plot, setting, conflict, theme, and personal reaction.

Next, *Research* three persons, places, or things mentioned in the story and present your findings to the class.

Finally, prepare a *Creative*, dramatic response to your story selection. Dramatize a scene from the story, create a new ending, or develop and act out a "meanwhile" scene.

The dramatic response in particular lends itself to ingenuity and personal expression. In my classroom, a dramatic response to "The Golden Honeymoon" by Ring Lardner resulted in an anniversary party complete with cake, punch, and a decorated "ballroom." Other possible dramatic responses are limited only by students' imagination.

For example, students might decide to dramatize the first meeting of Lucynell Crater with Mr. Shiftlet from Flannery O'Connor's short story "The Life You Save May Be Your Own." Students could note how their characters (as the reader later finds them) are revealed or obscured at this early point in the story.

Using Kurt Vonnegut, Jr.'s "Harrison Bergeron," students might further explore the story's theme by presenting a scene from a classroom in which everyone is made equal in "every which way." What kinds of adjustments to everyone's abilities would ensure equal achievement? What would the results be? Or, students might create a new story ending. What would happen if Harrison and his "Empress" had survived the Handicapper General's assault instead of dying?

As yet another possibility, students might decide to dramatize a "meanwhile" story based on the conclusion of Richard Wright's "The Man Who Was Almost a Man," in which the parents discover that Sammy has taken the unloaded gun and jumped a train heading North. What would they be saying at the same time he is congratulating himself on having acquired this new mastery over his destiny.

Whatever students choose to do, they are free to present either a videotaped or a live version of their production. A final mark for the presentation is a combination of teacher, peer, and self-evaluations. Students use class time to freely discuss or debate fine points of each story, within their groups or as a class, and these group discussions prove invaluable for reaching a communal understanding of each story.

I have used the *Critical, Research,* and *Creative* approach to short story seminars for the past six years. Students and teachers alike enjoy a different approach to prose fiction. And even more meaningful, students remember what they have seen and done.

Hendrik Smit, Lambton-Kent Composite School, Dresden, Ontario

MAPS IN THE ENGLISH CLASSROOM

"What do you teach?"
"Why do you have maps in an English classroom?"

These are two of the most common questions people ask when they walk into my classroom. Yet some of the most interesting geography and history mini-lessons take place in my English classroom. Students feel they get away from doing "real" work; I think it is time well spent. Two large, colorful, laminated maps (one of the United States and one of the world) decorate the back wall of my classroom all year. I consider these essential reference materials.

We refer to the maps constantly. As we discuss an author's background information, we point out and talk about some of the places mentioned in the biography. A collection of stories by O. Henry serves as a good example. His short stories involve a wide variety of settings and characters. By actually locating and highlighting (with water-based markers) some of the places O. Henry visited and gathered material, students gain a better understanding of the themes in many of his stories. When we read Mark Twain's memories of life along the Mississippi River, we discuss the importance of the location of the river itself and why Twain's writings have such appeal. A discussion about steamboats as a means of transportation in this area follows naturally. When we read Jack London's *The Call of the Wild*, we plot Buck's morbid adventure from sunny California to the fierce Northland. Students get a visual concept of the drastic change in environment as the plot progresses. A unit on Greek mythology provides a wonderful opportunity for locating distant deserts, mountain ranges, peaks, or seas that are the basis of these stories. A unit on historical fiction allows for discussion about the North and South during the Civil War or American colonies during the American Revolution. Invariably, a geography or history buff in every class will share in-depth information about a favorite topic. Several students who have traveled to, lived in, or vacationed at some of these spots proudly share firsthand information.

All this discussion serves as brainstorming, and produces ideas that eventually show up in some of our own writings. We use the maps to check the spelling of different places or look for distant lands as settings for our own stories. Students often come by during lunch to play trivia geography questions.

I keep maps in my English classroom because we use them. They are wonderful tools to teach geography, history, and English. Too many times we assume that all students possess basic geography or history knowledge. Many don't. We must use whatever visuals help students grasp concepts. As teachers, we can help students make the interdisciplinary connection.

Linda Siller, Lytle Junior High School, Lytle, Texas

CREATING CLASSROOM PLAYS FROM ADOLESCENT NOVELS

The cost involved in transforming a novel into a film is huge, and Hollywood is usually more concerned with whether the book will make money than with the themes of the story. As a class project, however, the process of converting a novel into a play can be exciting. Not only can the activity include many students in the production of a play, an activity usually reserved for only the more courageous of souls who venture onto the stage, but it can reinforce basic English skills in reading, writing, speaking, and editing.

Many novels for adolescents lend themselves readily to this adaptation process. Filled with dialogue, action, and themes young people identify with, these books are ideal for transformation to the stage. Also they are filled with people the same age as members of the class. It is much easier for young actors to play persons their own age than to pretend to be seventy years old. The problems of the characters, their hopes, dreams, failures and successes can easily be identified by most adolescent readers, and the young actors may be less self-conscious about how they look on stage.

Selection of the novel to be performed may be based on the following criteria: Is the theme important to the students at this school? How much rewriting is necessary? How long should the production last? A novel chosen by one of my classes at North Community High School in Minneapolis was Robert Cormier's *The Chocolate War*.

Why choose *The Chocolate War*? My reasons fit the above criteria. First, the book is filled with action. From the opening page of the novel, the plot moves quickly and consistently builds in intensity and tension toward the violent fight near the end. The reader is constantly wondering what will happen next. Second, the book is filled with dialogue that students used right off the page. We didn't have to spend too much time changing lines to fit the stage. Third, the theme itself, the individual standing up against a cold society, is an idea my students could quickly identify with. The class was a blend of average tenth through twelfth grade students. *The Chocolate War* with its focus on individuality and society gave enough material for all of the students. For tenth graders concerned with their own role in school the novel dealt with concern for individual problems. For twelfth graders the novel questioned ideals and values of the adult world into which they would soon graduate.

The first task after selection of the novel was simply to have the students sit down and read the book for enjoyment. There would be plenty of time after reading to find themes, ideas, characters, and the like. For the first time out, their primary task was to see if they enjoyed what they were reading. Since these books are usually no longer than two hundred pages, the students can read the book in three to five days. I assigned *The Chocolate War* on a Wednesday and the students and I began our discussions the following Monday, allowing the weekend to be part of the reading time. Once most of the students began reading the novel, they couldn't put it down. They had the book read within two days.

The second task was to discuss the book from three points of view. Did they enjoy the book? What were the major themes or ideas in the book? Who were the main characters? While this kind of discussion is common in most English classes, the discussions took on a whole new light because the students were almost literally going to bring these characters to life.

The fact that they enjoyed the book was imperative. Nothing could be worse for students than to work on a project they didn't enjoy. By "enjoy" I don't mean they necessarily had to like the book. One typical comment from a student was "I loved it, but I hated it at the same time." Further discussion revealed that the student found the actions of the characters unpleasant to read, but enjoyed the suspense and excitement of the book. A novel that is dull, or doesn't spark any real life in the class is doomed before the project even gets started. If the students are not enthusiastic about a book, a different one should be selected.

Looking at the themes of the novel becomes a practical matter, not an abstraction, nothing more than a test question or discussion topic. The theme becomes the backbone of the project. The students are going to be editing and selecting material for the novel. They must know, for their own benefit as well as the project, what they are ultimately trying to say in the play.

The discussions of *The Chocolate War* were spontaneous. Because the ending was not a clean and neat conclusion, the students found themselves looking at the nature of the characters and asking questions such as, "Did Jerry sell out? Did Archie really win at the end? Can an individual really stand up against popular opinion?" The theme must be clearly understood by the group in a project like this. It can be easy to fly off on tangents and lose the focus of the project. The theme locks the students into the task at hand, allowing them to question the actions of the charactors, but at the same time, keeping their focus true to the work.

The roles of each of the characters must be identified. The students need to know who the protagonist, the antagonist, secondary characters, and minor characters are. They don't have to be analyzed at this stage of the project, just identified. Once casting is done and the play goes into rehearsals, character analysis will become very important, but for now, just knowing basic facts about the characters is all that is necessary.

The third step in this process is the pre-editing exercise. In order to change the form of a work the students must have a full understanding of what they have to deal with in the first place: a chapter-by-chapter breakdown of what happens in the novel composed by the entire group. Notes should indicate when characters enter for the first time, how often they are mentioned, and how important they are to the overall outcome of the production.

Then the students edit the play. They must begin to think in a visual sense. They are converting a written work into a visual medium. A lot of what is being said in the book can be stated by gesture and stage composition. For example *The Chocolate War* begins with Jerry at football practice. We see that he is a tough kid and can take a lot of physical punishment. This is important, but at the same time, almost impractical for the stage. How can we solve the problem?

The second chapter presents Archie, the primary antagonist, and Obie, his stooge, discussing assignments for their secret organization, the Vigils. In that conversation they talk about Jerry, and Archie mentions how tough he is. For the stage we reverse these two chapters, or images. Archie and Obie began the play, introducing a dark, sinister mood, and Jerry entered after they had left and delivered a monologue about what happened at football practice. In this way, thinking in a visual sense, students learn the importance of dialogue and action in a play.

Another-problem can be scene changes. Often these novels have short chapters with quick changes in the location of the action. In novel form this is easy to deal with and the reader has no trouble jumping from one location to the next. In a play, however, too many jumps in location become confusing and, at times, irritating. What is necessary then is to blend as many scenes, or chapters, as possible into one location.

In *The Chocolate War*, a lot of the action is back and forth from one location to the next. The class, in editing the play, created only a few primary locations from the book: the football field, the Vigils' room, the classroom, and the hallway. In blending these locations, we had the action flow in and out of a particular room.

For example, roll calls are very important in the novel. Two of the roll calls are almost back to back, with a scene in Jerry's house breaking up the action. Do we get everybody off stage for the house scene and then back on for the second roll call? No. That would be too much of an interruption in the action. Instead we had the actors freeze on stage, Jerry gave a monologue to the audience, and then everybody went into the second roll call.

Once the basic pre-editing and editing were completed, the class literally tore apart a copy of the book, keeping bits of the dialogue and noting exposition that was going to be changed. Stage directions were kept to a minimum. Many beginning playwrights fall into the trap of writing stage direction after stage direction. A rule to remember is that dialogue and action carry out the requirements of a play. If the dialogue isn't doing the job properly, it should be fixed.

Anything the group had trouble converting into dialogue and action was changed through improvised scenes based on what was happening in the book. For example, chapter ten is almost entirely an internal monologue, inside Archie's mind. An improvisation based on what Archie was thinking brought out the exposition easily and condensed the chapter. This helped in two ways. First, it gave good insights to the characters in the book. The characters must stay true to themselves. Why did Archie act the way he did? What was his motivation? Second, every character, even Archie, thinks he is justified in his actions. Right or wrong, the action had to be justified.

Once a script is organized—not completed, but organized—the cast should sit down and read it aloud to one another. This can be a frightening moment. Lines that sound fine when read silently can sound terrible out loud. A member of the group should underline portions of the script that sound stilted. The class should remember that no script sounds wonderful the first time out and even Shakespeare had his off days. With rehearsals and a good ear, the script will grow.

Costumes can be kept simple. Since *The Chocolate War* takes place at a private school, we needed uniforms. We went to a used clothing outlet and found a dozen school uniforms at cut-rate prices.

Subtle costumes changes and voice changes suggested a change in characters. Sets were kept to a minimum. We used only folding chairs to help suggest different locations. The focus of a play like this should always be on the characters. With constant work on the script, often up to the final weeks of rehearsals, set construction can get in the way of the work.

We kept *The Chocolate War* short, the length of one class period. We also held discussions after each performance. Young people who had spent six weeks trying to be as nasty as Archie or as brave as Jerry or as rotten as Brother Leon should have some interesting insights into these characters that they share with a group.

This project gives students clearer insights into a book than a class discussion or a book report. Creating plays out of novels is a lot of work, but it is also a lot of fun. Basic English skills are given a practical focus, and in the end the students will have a product they can truly claim as their own.

Michael Kennedy, North Community High School, Minneapolis, Minnesota

Threads of Life
READING, WRITING, AND MUSIC

It is June, and the night before the last day of school. There are 150 seventh graders performing their original musical for more than 300 parents, teachers, and other students. We are packed elbow to elbow. We have created a makeshift theater-in-the-round from the gymnasium in our middle school. I am behind the audience attempting to keep 149 members of the cast relatively quiet, despite the stifling heat. Sweat runs down my arms, drips off my elbows, my eyebrows, my nose. The lingering odors from years of basketball and volleyball games hang heavy. Hundreds of play programs fan the still air. Dave, the music teacher, strikes a chord on the piano, as Josh joins in on guitar. Scene 3, A dim spotlight finds Matt, a seventh grader who often can't answer his biggest question about school, "What's this for?" Tonight he is playing the role of Rico. It is the 1990s. Rico, a high school student and the head of a gang known as the Pounders, is alone in an abandoned textile mill. Alone and hiding. Blamed for a crime he didn't commit. He opens his mouth and sings:

> *I sometimes wonder what happened to me.*
> *I was left alone, dropped on the street.*
> *Just eight years old; left to fend for myself.*
> *Nothing really matters, not even life itself.*
>
> *This is my life. This is how it goes.*
> *When you live the way that I do*
> *You get used to the blows.*
> *But somethin's goin' down,*
> *Someone's got to fall.*
> *This is my life, up against the wall . . .*

For several seconds after Matt stops singing, I notice that the whole room is holding its breath. Then it exhales into thunderous applause. Matt, too, exhales. It is no easy task singing a solo in front of one's peers, especially when you have never sung, or acted, or wanted to. And this is no easy song. It is laden with emotion, laden with high notes. But Matt hits them all. It doesn't matter that it's June, or that it's the night before the last day of school. For the first time in seventh grade, Matt has his answer to "What's it for?" And not just Matt. As the lights come up, I notice Alyssa and Julie. They are rows apart but find each other's eyes. They, too, know the answer. They wrote the lyrics to this song.

For years, Dave Ervin, the music teacher, and I talked about planning a project together, believing that what the seventh graders could do in one class would be doubly enhanced if they were guided through it in two classes. But we never found the time to design a plan. We admitted finally that we would never find the time. "Let's just do it," we said. We believed, but never said out loud, that our similar philosophical beliefs would guide us through this project.

Music, like writing, is a mode of expression that attempts to describe those things that we do not yet understand. In both the music and language arts classes, we are asking students to raise the questions that a text brings to mind. What surprises you? Perplexes you? What do you want to know more about? The text may be a novel, a poem, a song, an essay, a picture, one's own writing, or an observation of the world around you. In this case, their answers to these questions took the shape of narrative scripts, lyrics, and music.

In order for any form of expression to have value, it must be meaningful, purposeful, and enriching.

- Meaning is that which makes an intellectual and emotional connection with the learner.
- Purpose is that which leads the learner from one meaning to another.
- Enrichment is that which gives the learner a deeper understanding of herself or himself, others, and the world.

Both of us strive to make those experiences we offer our students meaningful, purposeful, and enriching. We know that about each other.

I wanted to teach the seventh graders how to conduct research. Dave wanted them to write and perform an original musical. Both of us wanted as many students as possible to find success in many different ways. Both of us wanted them to have fun.

In language arts classes, students concentrated on the drafting and refining of a story, the turning of a narrative into a script, the language of the characters, and the drafting of poetry for lyrics. In music classes, Dave also guided them through the development and refinement of the story, the refining of the scripts, the refinement of the lyrics, and setting the lyrics to music. Could we work collaboratively with little planning and a lot of intuition and trust to guide us? We had six weeks to find out.

IN LANGUAGE ARTS

I have two basic purposes for teaching research skills. I want the students to really learn about something in depth—something that is meaningful, purposeful, and enriching—and I want them to leave my classroom knowing how to learn. I learn best when I have some input into what I will learn. Our students need to be given that same option. There are times, however, when I like to be pushed in directions I might not choose for myself. I think there are times when we need to set some of those same parameters for our students. It pushes their thinking.

For most of the year, students had read books of their own choosing. Although we had read numerous short stories, poetry, journalism articles, and picture books together, we had not read a novel as a whole class. Since individuals read in a variety of ways, I offer students all those possibilities.

This time, I wanted all of us to read and respond to a novel together. Too often we choose books to read together with a male protagonist, so I wanted the main character to be a girl, one who is feisty despite the odds. I wanted the book to be fresh, new to me also. And I wanted the book to be historical fiction, because I've noticed few students choose it for themselves.

Most important, we had to consider our constraints of time and numbers. We had 150 students brainstorming ideas for a musical. We had six weeks in which to make it happen. All 150 students had to be part of the performance on stage. We needed to confine the topic for our sake as teachers, as well as for the students. We decided that the research would focus on the mills during the Industrial Revolution. We would have the students read *Lyddie* by Katherine Paterson, we would take them to the Boott Mill in Lowell, Massachusetts, and we would ask them to write a musical based on their wonderings and findings. I wanted the students to respond to this reading in more than a personal way. I wanted them to take apart the layers of this novel, and construct their own meaning through a new medium, one that was unfamiliar to them and me—in this case, a musical.

Reading *Lyddie*

Before reading *Lyddie*, I asked the students to take three minutes to jot down in their journals everything they knew about mills in New England or the Industrial Revolution. After just thirty seconds they were looking around the room staring at each other. They knew little. My list wasn't much longer. I would be learning right along with them.

After reading the first chapter, I was hooked. I read a few passages to the students. They wanted to hear more. Students bought their own copies. (I provided books to those students who couldn't afford it.) I wanted them to write in the margins, underline, question, react . . . .

I gave the students eight days to read *Lyddie*—about three chapters, or twenty-five pages a night. I asked them to make notations in their books by underlining, starring, or bracketing key phrases or paragraphs that would be helpful to them in developing characters, writing dialogue and scenes, and understanding relationships during this time period. I asked them specifically to note (in their books or in their journals):

- personal reaction to each night's reading
- examples of language and/or expressions that you would most likely not use or hear today:

  "Oh Lord, deliver us!" (p. 2)
  "You want I should go with you as far as the village?" (p. 6)
  She minded mightily being beholden. (p. 7)

- metaphors and similes that described situations, places, or people:

  Lyddie could feel the rage oozing up like sap on a March morning. (p. 20)
  Mistress Cutler watched Lyddie like a barn cat on a sparrow . . . (p. 24)
  Missing Charlie was like wearing a stone around her neck. (p. 24)
  Fatigue was like a toothache in her bones. (p. 138)

- descriptions that stick with you/bring things to mind for you:

    A factory was a hundred stagecoaches all inside one's skull, banging their wheels against the bone. (p.63)

- examples of ways young women were treated, and expected to behave
- conditions on the farms, in the mills, in the boardinghouses
- things you notice about Lyddie:

    issues/problems/people Lyddie must contend with
    ways she handles herself
    characteristics you admire in Lyddie
    the significant messages you take away from Lyddie's story

- questions that come to mind as you read

I read with the students, often starting each day with a passage I loved (or hated), talking about what they and I had discovered, giving them time to read, and sometimes asking them to try a quick-write. Over the course of two weeks, I asked the students to write for three to five minutes in their journals in each of these ways:

- Draft a letter as a mill girl to four different audiences—a family member, a best friend, the overseer, and the newspaper— about what it's like in the mills.
- Pour out a journal entry as if you are loving or hating your newfound "freedom" as a factory worker (conditions, expectations, treatment, hopes, dreams).
- Draft a petition to the overseer about the conditions you can no longer tolerate (make suggestions about what might be done better).
- Read pages 74–80 again. What does reading mean to you?

All of this reading and writing was to connect them with the time period—immerse them in the language, sensitize them to the issues, encourage them to feel the emotions of real people. They were sketching out ideas every time they read and wrote, not knowing where or when those ideas would find their way into song lyrics, a setting, a script.

Krista drafted a diary entry for one quick-write. Part of it said: "I shar a room with six other girls. We are so cramped its like putting all six of us into one set of clothing. Wone girl has a cof and won't see a docter. I heer her nite after nite hacking like a sik cow . . . ."

After finishing the book, she wrote in her journal, "*Lyddie* was one of the best books I've ever read . . . . I'm not sure if you noticed, but I wrote all of my favorite quotes in my log instead of the book because I treasure the book and I would like to pass it on to my children . . . .This book really gave me a 'flavor' of the 1800s and helped a lot in writing the play. I felt like I really learned something. History is not one of my favorite things to study, but I'm really into what we are doing in L.A. and music . . . . My absolute favorite quote in the whole book was [after Lyddie crammed the fire bucket over Mr. Marsden's head for what he was doing to Brigid], 'Behind in the darkness, she thought she heard the noise of an angry bear crashing an oatmeal pot against the furniture' (p. 161). It seems that that was what the whole book *Lyddie* was about."

Once students finished reading *Lyddie* as a whole class, I expected them to continue reading and responding in their journals to additional recommended titles. (See References.) This worked especially well for those students who read *Lyddie* in a day or two and wanted more to read. I also read several books aloud: *The Lorax* by Dr. Seuss, *Mill* by David Macauley, and *A River Ran Wild* by Lynne Cherry.

As they read, the students wanted to know more.

"How come the girls left their farms to work in such awful places?"
"Were the mills really that bad?"
"How come they worked under such horrible conditions?"
"Why were they treated so terribly? How could the overseers get away with that?"
"Why were there only girls working in the mills?"

To help students in their search for answers, we took them to the reconstructed textile mills in Lowell, Massachusetts. After working on hand looms, listening first hand to the deafening clatter of actual machines, and learning about the working conditions, we returned to our classrooms. In language arts classes, I asked the students, "What surprised you? What do you want to know more about?" Their answers, in the form of questions, surprised me. "Do you think the ghost of Lizzie Ryan still haunts the mill?" "How did they stand the noise of those machines?" "How did they breathe with all that dust around?" "Why didn't they protest?" "How come they didn't just go back to the farm?"

The park ranger who had acted as our guide had told the story of a girl named Lizzie Ryan. The students remembered every detail. She was a real mill girl in the 1800s. She died when she fell five stories while trying to slide down the bannister for a quick retreat to supper. Supposedly "her ghost still haunts the Boott Mill," the ranger said.

During their tour through Lowell on the old trolley car, students noticed groups of students hanging out behind the present-day high school near the mill. High schoolers seemed to congregate in definite ethnic groups. To our seventh graders, these groups of older students were intimidating. For days, their talk always circled back to Lizzie's ghost and the gangs of high schoolers. As we formulated questions for our research, "What we want to know more about," ideas seemed to head in those two distinct directions.

What if Lizzie really did haunt the mills? What if she could come back to life? What would she be like? Would she fit in? Why would she haunt the mills? How could she come back to life? What would she be like if she did? What would she find today?

Were those real gangs hanging out behind the high school? How were they divided up? What are their lives like? Is each gang different? What would have happened if someone had taunted them? Would they have tried to hurt us? Are these the great-grandchildren of the men and women who were immigrants in the 1800s? Are these the descendants of the boys and girls who came off the farms to work in the mills? Were these kids new immigrants?

In their research, reading, and writing, the students continued to return again and again to their own questions about Lizzie Ryan and about gangs. The students' questions about conditions in the mills, their continued interest as we read *Lyddie*, and their curiosity about gangs indicated there was enough interest to sustain their research. In both language arts and music classes we asked the students to focus their ideas for a story around the Industrial Revolution, concentrating particularly on its effect on women in the mill towns. We had no idea how their interest in gangs might connect, or even if it would connect at all.

IN MUSIC CLASS

The drafting of story ideas began in Dave's music class with "What ifs?" The students' "What ifs?" ran the gamut from aliens having root canals in a dentist's outer space office to a former mill worker being born again as a cowboy. Although no "What if?" was wrong, only the ones that could be built upon from student to student ever survived the process. The students kept going back to the ghost of Lizzie Ryan and today's gangs in cities. The focus began to become clearer as one class went around the room:

> What if a Hispanic gang in 1993 is accused of killing another gang's leader? What if they run to the abandoned mill and hide? What if they hear police sirens and quickly get into an old elevator? What if the elevator suddenly jerks to a start and they're carried into the past when the mills were working? What if a member of the gang doesn't want to leave the past? What if the gang members are expected to work? What if they form a strike? What if one of them is killed by a machine? What if they try to take the mill workers

with them back to the present? What if one of the mill workers looks, talks, and acts like one of the gang members?

The "What ifs?" continued in music classes for several days until the students had the beginning of a story that had to do with the ghost of Lizzie Ryan from the mills and something to do with gangs of today. Those ideas came back to the language arts classes where I had students break into two groups: those who wanted to focus on ideas that had to do with Lizzie Ryan, and those who wanted to discuss possibilities associated with the gangs. We then brainstormed ways of connecting the two. Once we had the connection, students broke into groups of three to five to come up with an outline for a whole story. Ideas were shared with the whole class; the best-liked ideas went down to music classes where they were further refined. Once we had an outline, we broke it into six scenes (some clearer than others), giving the responsibility for developing each scene to an entire class of seventh graders (we had six sections of seventh graders).

PRODUCING THE MUSICAL

Refining the Script in Language Arts

Once we had a scene for each class, I broke the students into groups of three to five, gave them a brief summary of the scene, and asked them to write a one-to-three page narration which they then turned into a three-to-five page script. Each group read their parts as they acted out their scenes. We voted on the most effective ones, attempting to combine the best from each. Minilessons included the following: setting the scene; turning narration into dialogue; refining dialogue based on language of the time, character, and need; writing narration; writing description; finding appropriate places for songs; writing poetry/lyrics; rhyming; writing effective titles; and use of literary devices (such as metaphor and simile).

Of the six seventh-grade language arts classes, I had only two of them. The four I did not have worked on this musical with David only. My entire 50-minute period with my two classes was devoted to researching and writing their scripts and songs. At night, I often took the rough-draft scripts from the other four classes home to give them my written response, questions, and suggestions. I listened to their songs after school, and offered my response in a similar fashion.

One of my classes was responsible for the opening mill scene; the other was responsible for a contemporary classroom scene. Unfortunately, we had little time to read about inner-city gangs. In the class responsible for the gang scene, I did read several passages from *The Outsiders* by S. E. Hinton, and asked the students to listen to the news and clip articles from newspapers for any information about gang-related incidents. I asked them to pay specific attention to the attitudes of the gang members, if they were able to glean that kind of information. I also had these students do several quick-writes in their journals, using the prompt, "As a gang member, draft a letter to your best friend, your worst enemy, a teacher, a family member, and a potential employer about what life is like for you in the inner city."

I cut out every article I could find and posted significant stories. I related a story to the students about why collecting research was so important to understanding a character, especially one that might be difficult to relate to. In 1988, while on a fellowship at the Kennedy Center in Washington, D.C., I met Victoria Clark after her performance as Madame Thenardier, the tavern owner's wife, in *Les Miserables*. In order to understand her role as a "child abuser," she kept an artistic journal in which she collected every article or passage she could find (from life and literature) that related to abusive treatment of children, so that she could understand the emotional, psychological, and physical aspects of such a character. If there had been more time, we should have spent it on reading so much more about gangs—who the kids are, what their lives are like, why they need the gangs, how they talk, what they do and do not value, how violence is a part of their lives, etc. But we had less than a week to finish the scripts. We worked with what the students knew.

As we worked on the scripts, I found the most difficult part was trying to keep all twenty-five students in each class completely occupied with the scripts or songwriting. It did not always work. Some students were completely committed to the tasks. Others lost interest once the initial script was written. Because there were no props or sets for the production, there was little else for these students to do.

Casting Parts in Music

Once we had the six scenes, we figured out who the main characters were. In music classes, David used two rough draft songs (one about the mills, the other about gangs) for auditions. Anyone could audition for any part. Every student in the class then voted on which two or three students should get a callback. At callbacks, the three students from every class who received the most votes tried out using the same two rough draft songs. Two students from each section, who didn't want to try out, ranked the students. After the session, David and I held a closed-door discussion with the selection committee. We went around the room. We each voted on one person who we thought absolutely had to have a major role. We could name someone who had been named or someone different. Then we listed the best student from each section, based on strength and quality of voice, ability to portray a particular character, ability to connect with the audience, etc. The only requirements that had to be met were these: there must be one major role in each seventh-grade section, and there must be a balance of girls and boys in major roles. Being fair is more important in seventh grade than always giving the lead to the very best because the best is often the same person year after year. We have to be more trusting that kids will rise to the occasion when given an opportunity that really challenges them. So often they do.

Scripts and songs were refined and polished like any piece of writing: readers (students and teachers) continually pointed out the places that worked or stuck with them; asked questions to refine the pace, the accuracy of the language, or the story; and made suggestions.

Setting Text to Music

Dave Ervin *is* what he teaches: a musician, a composer, and a singer. He holds high standards for kids, and they know it. He puts great trust in them. But he also teaches them. He believes that singing is natural in all of us: that we start life singing before we even begin to talk. We almost have to *learn* to talk, to speak *without* pitch. Therefore, his job is to encourage students not to fear uttering pitched sounds again. He also believes that music is a language of emotion; the music behind words is there to make the emotion of those words more understandable. Setting words to music means convincing kids of those two premises.

Dave has found a process that helps kids take their words, find the emotion in them, and discover the music that is already there. He:

- has the students break the text into word groups, phrases, and/or sentences.
- has the students explore the meaning and emotion of the phrase or word group through speech, saying it over and over dozens of times until they feel ready to perform the line in a play.
- has the students add more and more pitch to their speech, as if they were giving an impassioned soap box sermon. He continually reminds them, however, not to change the meaning. They must only add pitch to their speech.
- has the students discover the notes and rhythms of the line.
- and finally, helps them to set an accompaniment to their melody.

Once kids speak their lines in an emotionally clear way, the music is almost there. The trick is to get kids to say the words until they get the exact emotion, which takes a lot of trust in a safe environment. David creates this environment by accepting all that kids say and do with ideas. He helps them see how they could be better. Once the kids' words connect with their emotion, they can begin to hear the notes. As David explains, "If students see the text without doing this, it rarely makes the meaning and emotion of the words more understandable. At best, they create beautiful words attached to beautiful but unrelated music. At worst, it is beautiful words that are caged within a nursery school melody, canceling out all real emotion."

In music classes and after school, David worked with the students who had major roles. He also helped the students who wrote the songs through this process by orchestrating and arranging the music so that it fit the mood, the character, the story, and the lyrics. All of the lyrics, musical scores, and scripts were written by students with our guidance and suggestions.

Because every seventh grader was in the production, older students accompanied on piano, guitar, and other musical instruments. There were no props. With twenty-five students frequently on stage, props got in the way. Students used hand motions, facial expressions, and body language to indicate various props. Costumes were simplified also: homespun for the mill girls, different colored T-shirts for the gang members. At various points during the production, slides of the mills were flashed on all four walls of the gymnasium.

REFLECTION

This kind of project was not an easy task. There were many times during the six weeks that I asked myself, "What am I doing this for?" But the production itself, still a rough draft, was testament to the entire process. When that whole room exhaled into thunderous applause for Matt, I knew exactly what David and I were doing this for. It's always for Matt, and Rachel, and Casey, and Jeanne, and Jeremy, and Alyssa, and . . . . It's for all those reasons. And they all have names.

In *Lyddie*, Katherine Paterson says, "The next day in the mill, the noise was just as jarring and her feet in Triphena's old boots swelled just as large, but now and again she caught herself humming . . . . Tonight after supper, Betsy would read to her again . . . . there was a delicious anticipation, like molded sugar on her tongue . . . . it wasn't so much that she had gotten used to the mill, but she had found a way to escape its grasp. The pasted sheets of poetry or Scripture in the window frames, the geraniums on the sill, those must be some other girl's way, she decided. But hers was a story." (p. 79)

For many students, school tends to be as jarring as those mills. We have to find ways of helping them put "geraniums on the sills." We have to recognize that it is our job to find meaningful, purposeful, enriching ways of learning with which kids can connect. We have to offer students all of these same opportunities for responding to "story." Some write, some sing, some listen. They all need to read. And pushing their thinking beyond just personal, immediate response, helps them understand not only themselves, but others. Through reading, writing, and music, students were truly reflecting on their responses to literature and all that it encompasses. Like Matt, they found themselves humming. What better response can we get from readers?

REFERENCES

Cherry, L. (1992). *A River Ran Wild*. Orlando, FL: Harcourt Brace.

Hinton, S. E. (1967). *The Outsiders*. New York: Dell.

Hugo, V. [1887] (1961). *Les Miserables*. New York: Fawcett.

Macaulay, D. (1989). *Mill*. Boston, MA: Houghton Mifflin.

Paterson, K (1991). *Lyddie*. New York: Dutton Child Books.

Rosenblatt, L. M. (1983). *Literature as Exploration*. (4th ed.). New York: MLA.

Seuss, Dr. (1971). *The Lorax*. New York: Random Books for Young Readers.

RECOMMENDED READING

Collier, J. L., & Collier, C. (1992) . *The Clock*. New York: Delacorte.

Dublin, T. (1981). *Farm to Factory: Women's Letters 1830–1860*. New York: Columbia University Press.

Larcom, L. (1961). *A New England Girlhood*. Gloucester, MA: Peter Smith.

Lord, A. (1981). *A Spirit to Ride the Whirlwind*. New York: Macmillan.

Robinson, H. H. (1976). *Loom and Spindle*. Kailua, HI: Press Pacifica.

Weisman, J. B. (Ed.). (1991). *The Lowell Mill Girls: Life in the Factories*. Lowell, MA Enterprises.

Linda Rief with David Ervin, Oyster River Middle School, Durham, New Hampshire

Other NCTE Books about English Language Arts Standards

Any of the useful resources described below can be ordered from the National Council of Teachers of English by phoning 1-800-369-6283; by faxing your order to 1-217-328-9645; by emailing your order request to <kkesler@ncte.org>; or by sending your order to NCTE Order Fulfillment, 1111 W. Kenyon Road, Urbana, IL 61801-1096.

To preview these resources, visit the NCTE home page at <http://www.ncte.org>.

Standards for the English Language Arts
FROM THE NATIONAL COUNCIL OF TEACHERS OF ENGLISH AND THE INTERNATIONAL READING ASSOCIATION

What should English language arts students know and be able to do? This book—the culmination of more than three years of intense research and discussion among members of the English language arts teaching community, parents, and policymakers—answers this question by presenting standards that encompass the use of print, oral, and visual language and addresses six interrelated English language arts: reading, writing, speaking, listening, viewing, and visually representing. *Standards for the English Language Arts* starts by examining the rationale for standard setting—why NCTE and IRA believe defining standards is important and what we hope to accomplish by doing so. The book then explores the assumptions that underlie the standards, defines and elaborates each standard individually, and provides real-life classroom vignettes in which readers can glimpse standards in practice. Designed to complement state and local standards efforts, this document will help educators prepare *all* K–12 students for the literacy demands of the twenty-first century. 1996. Grades K–12. ISBN 0-8141-4676-7.

Stock No. 46767-4025
$18.00 nonmembers
$13.00 NCTE members

Standards in Practice Series

Written with the classroom teacher in mind, these resources have been developed by experienced educators to illustrate how students, teachers, parents, and schools can work together to achieve higher literacy standards. These books offer rich classroom portraits that demonstrate how enlightened thinking about teaching and learning can foster student achievement in each of the language arts—reading, writing, speaking, listening, viewing, and visually representing—through rigorous study that is driven by students' inquiry into the world around them. Keyed to grade-level ranges, these practical resources are designed as a complement to *Standards for the English Language Arts* and will support teachers and administrators as they help each student develop the English language arts skills and abilities to succeed in the coming century.

Standards in Practice, Grades K–2
by Linda K. Crafton
(ISBN 0-8141-4691-0)
Stock No. 46910-4025
$15.95 nonmembers
$11.95 NCTE members

Standards in Practice, Grades 3–5
by Martha Sierra-Perry
(ISBN 0-8141-4693-7)
Stock No. 46937-4025
$15.95 nonmembers
$11.95 NCTE members

Standards in Practice, Grades 6–8
by Jeffrey D. Wilhelm
(ISBN 0-8141-4694-5)
Stock No. 46945-4025
$15.95 nonmembers
$11.95 NCTE members

Standards in Practice, Grades 9–12
by Peter Smagorinsky
(ISBN 0-8141-4695-3)
Stock No. 46953-4025
$15.95 nonmembers
$11.95 NCTE members

Additional Titles in the Standards Consensus Series

*Teaching the Writing Process
in High School*
(ISBN 0-8141-5286-4)
Stock No. 52864-4025
$12.95 nonmembers
$9.95 NCTE members

*Teaching Literature in
High School: The Novel*
(ISBN 0-8141-5282-1)
Stock No. 52821-4025
$12.95 nonmembers
$9.95 NCTE members

*Motivating Writing in
Middle School*
(ISBN 0-8141-5287-2)
Stock No. 52872-4025
$12.95 nonmembers
$9.95 NCTE members